GRATEFUL TO HAVE BEEN THERE

My 42 Years with Bill and Lois,
and the Evolution of Alcoholics Anonymous

BY NELL WING

PARKSIDE Publishing Corporation

205 West Touhy Avenue
Park Ridge, Illinois 60068

The views expressed in this manuscript are based on the recollections of the author, and nothing contained herein is intended to imply approval or endorsement by Alcoholics Anonymous.

Grateful to Have Been There

ISBN 0-942421-44-2

Printed in the United States of America

10 9 8 7 6 5 4 3 2

In memory of
Bill and Lois W.
with love and gratitude for their
long and cherished friendship

CONTENTS

ACKNOWLEDGMENTS

I wish to express grateful thanks to the following for their helpfulness and support and for allowing me access to materials pertaining to A.A. history with permission to reprint from them:

The General Service Office of A.A.
A.A. World Services, Inc.
The A.A. Grapevine, Inc.
Al-Anon Family Group Headquarters, Inc.

In particular, I am grateful for the help of the A.A. Archives at G.S.O., the archivist, and A.A. World Services, Inc., for allowing me access to books, pamphlets, letters, and magazines. I also value deeply the sharing of personal memories by my friends who were former employees at the General Service Office of A.A.

I am grateful to the A.A. Grapevine, Inc. for sharing source information and permission to reprint.

I extend special thanks to Al-Anon Family Group Headquarters, Inc., for their cooperation in reviewing material pertaining to Lois W. and for permission to use portions of it.

I wish to express special thanks to Mrs. Lucille Kahn, for sharing her memories of meetings with Bill, Gerald Heard, and Aldous Huxley, at her and her husband's apartment in New York City.

I am grateful for the help and guidance of Bob P. in

collating and preparing the original materials and to so many of my long-time A.A. friends, who so graciously shared their memories of Bill and Lois with me.

And, finally, I thank the editors of Parkside Publishing for their helpful editing and preparation of the book itself.

PREFACE

For 20 years, Nell Wing was executive secretary and assistant to Bill W., cofounder of Alcoholics Anonymous. She remained a close friend and long-time companion to Lois W., cofounder of Al-Anon, for 17 more years after Bill's death. "They were my family," she says, and indeed, no one else has approached the warm and close relationship she enjoyed with these two most extraordinary figures.

She worked at the General Service Office of A.A. in New York City, from 1947 until her retirement at the end of 1982, starting as secretary-receptionist, and later serving as secretary to the A.A. World Services, Inc., Board. Later on, she assumed several General Service Conference duties, including the layout and production of the annual Conference Report. She also served several years as publications editor. During the last ten years of her service, she was the archivist for A.A.

No other living person knows more about how Alcoholics Anonymous developed and how it grew. No other living person has been as close and perceptive an observer of the excitement, the turbulence, and the spiritual underpinnings of what may be the most important social movement of the Twentieth Century.

In this book, she shares her memories and impressions of those watershed years.

1

MIAMI 1971

We were aboard a Lear jet chartered by Bill's good friend, Brinkley Smithers, to take Bill W. from his home in Bedford Hills, New York, to the Miami Heart Clinic in Miami, Florida. It was January 24, 1971. Bill, dreadfully ill, lay on a stretcher laid across the backs of several seats, wearing his oxygen mask. Lois sat at Bill's head, I sat nearby, and Dr. Ed B., his physician, was at his side, closely monitoring Bill's deteriorating condition.

As we flew, Bill slipped in and out of hallucinations, seeing dead or absent relatives at his feet. His left arm on occasion slipped off the narrow stretcher, and when I would lift it back onto his lap, he tried to smile and say thanks. "Hold fast," I said. It was one of Bill's favorite expressions.

The evening before, Lois and I were sitting in the library outside the upstairs bedroom at Stepping Stones, their home in Bedford Hills, New York, when Bill called out for a drink of water. The night aide, due at nine o'clock, had not yet arrived, so I fetched him a glass and cradled his head so he could drink it. Swallowing too quickly, he started to choke. I thought, "My God, we'll lose him right here!" But just then we heard a car rush up the driveway. The night aide hurried in and knew just what to do. Sensing he would be needed, he said, he had decided to come in early.

The next morning, the arranged-for ambulance arrived at Stepping Stones to pick up Bill and by early afternoon we were waiting for what seemed an eternity for the airplane to arrive from Miami at the Westchester County Airport in White Plains, New York. Bill was in the nearby ambulance, requiring constant attention, and Lois paced about anxiously, searching the sky for the tardy plane. Just as the aides were about to take Bill back to the Westchester hospital, the Lear jet arrived with Dr. Ed. We boarded and took off.

In Miami, we were met by A.A.s and driven to the Miami Heart Clinic, where we left Bill. Lois and I checked into separate rooms at a nearby motel, had a bite to eat, and fell into our beds.

At about 12:30 a.m., Ed called to tell me Bill was dead. He had died at 11:30 p.m., on January 24, 1971—53 years from the day he had married Lois. A.A. had lost its cofounder, Lois had lost her beloved husband, and I had lost my close friend and confidant, the big brother / father figure of my middle life. My own mother had died just a week and a half earlier.

Before awakening me, Ed had called Bob H., general manager of the General Service Office in New York, who set into motion a preplanned procedure for notifying everyone who needed to know, both in and out of Alcoholics Anonymous. About 1:00 a.m. Ed and others joined me in my room for what turned out to be an all-night vigil, every few minutes debating whether or not to wake Lois and tell her—but deciding each time to let her sleep a little longer, knowing the depth of her exhaustion and how much worse it was going to be for her in the immediate future.

About 6:30 a.m. we heard her stirring in the next room. Ed broke the news to her and she collapsed into his arms. To the end of her life Lois would harbor anger that the hospital hadn't notified her immediately of Bill's turn for the worse, so she could have been with him, and, understandably, that we hadn't told her immediately of his passing.

Bill loved his native Vermont and wished to be buried there beside other members of his family, but until the New England frozen earth had thawed sufficiently for the internment, his body was kept in storage in Miami, in a Vermont oak casket, arranged for by Dr. Ed. Burial took place on May 8 in East Dorset, Vermont, with a small group of family and friends present.

On January 26, the *New York Times* ran a front-page obituary with a picture of Bill. It continued for several columns inside. Hundreds of other newspapers around the world followed suit. These fill three scrapbooks in the A.A. Archives today. The world knew for the first time the full identity of the man who had, with Dr. Bob S., started Alcoholics Anonymous. On February 14, St. Valentine's Day, special memorial services were held in the Cathedral of St. John the Divine in New York, across the United States and Canada, in London, Antwerp, Bombay, Dublin, Glasgow, Johannesburg, Melbourne, Oslo, Istanbul, Sri Lanka, and Tokyo, throughout Central and South America, and in East Dorset, Vermont. At Stepping Stones, we had held a private service a few days earlier.

Back at A.A.'s General Service Office (G.S.O.), I began cleaning out the office Bill and I shared and tending to his posthumous affairs. There wasn't a lot to handle because plans had been made well in advance. But I was busy

3

enough organizing his papers, talks, and files. These duties, and many others, evolved into my job as archivist for the Fellowship, which I held until I retired at the end of 1982.

Though Bill was gone, his death was the beginning for me of an even closer companionship with Lois, which lasted until her death seventeen years later. My every-other-weekend visits to Stepping Stones continued, and my relationship with Lois grew into one I shall always cherish.

2

AND THIS IS BILL

My long journey with the A.A. Fellowship and Bill and Lois began on the cold, blustery morning of Monday, March 3, 1947, when I showed up at the A.A. office (at that time called the Alcoholic Foundation) at 415 Lexington Avenue, just across from Grand Central Station. It was a small office with about thirteen employees, including two staff members, and Bill, when he came down from Bedford Hills once a week.

I was introduced to Charlotte L., who was quite new herself at the office. After a brief chat, Charlotte guided me over to Marion Weaver, the office manager, who was even newer on the job. Marion told me that my salary would be small but that the spiritual rewards of the job, the satisfaction of helping people, would be great. I went to work immediately. Alcoholics Anonymous was not quite 12 years old; I was 29.

Actually, I knew a bit about A.A. before I came to the office. I have a very clear memory of sitting on the bed in my room at Keuka College in central New York State in late September, 1939, reading the article in *Liberty* magazine by Morris Markey entitled "Alcoholics and God."

A.A. was described very favorably, but I remember I wasn't very optimistic about its future. Being in my agnostic phase, I thought its emphasis on a Higher Power was a fatal mistake. I had also read the March 1941 *Saturday Evening Post* article, as well as other magazine articles, including two very good ones in *Reader's Digest*. These had always intrigued me.

After college and a very short career of teaching in a Mexican high school in my mother's hometown of San Antonio, Texas, I returned to Rochester, New York, did some secretarial work, and then joined the female wing of the Coast Guard, the SPARS, in 1944. I was sent to Lake Worth, Florida, for boot camp, and then was stationed in Seattle, Washington, for about two years.

Discharged at the end of the war, I was a bit of a nonconformist. There was a lot of movement around the country, especially during the latter part of the decade. The war was disruptive, lives were unsettled, and ideas changed, especially for women, who during the war years took over a lot of jobs normally suited to men. New vistas opened up for women during that time and the spirit to travel hit a lot of families and individuals, including me.

Not involved in any serious relationship and having a talent for art and sculpture, I thought it would be a good time to head for Mexico to study under a famous sculptor who taught at the American University in San Miguel de Allende, just above Mexico City. I was also intrigued by the idea of living a kind of Bohemian life with the international set in the area and the students at the university. I hadn't really planned out a specific schedule to get down there but I knew I needed a lot more money than my severance pay from the Coast Guard.

So I took the train down to New York City and located an employment agency. The interviewer studied my resume. Then she leaned close and whispered, "How would you like to work at Alcoholics Anonymous?" Not anticipating my enthusiastic answer, she almost fell off the chair. So it was, on Monday morning, March 3, 1947, a new life began for me when I knocked on the door, on the eleventh floor of 415 Lexington Avenue.

The next day, Tuesday, Bill W. appeared in the office. His usual pattern then, and to the end of his life, was to spend one or two days a week in town. Charlotte or Bobbie, I'm not sure which, took me over to his desk and left me, saying, "And this is Bill." I expected the usual amenities, but, truthfully, I'm not sure he even said hello. He eased his long, lanky frame onto a straight-backed chair, leaned way back (a habit I was to become familiar with over the years), crossed his legs, and immediately launched into a long monologue, talking about how the trustees were trying to keep him isolated in a kind of ivory tower, suggesting he ought to concentrate on just writing for the Fellowship. He went on about the need for something called the Traditions and for a general service conference made up of people from all over the country who would come to New York and help make decisions. I listened with all the interest I could muster, but I didn't really have the vaguest idea of what he was talking about. As I remember, I escaped as soon as I decently could.

But I learned two characteristics about Bill: one, he was not much given to small talk—that is, unless you introduced a subject in which he was particularly interested. In that case, it might be difficult to make your exit. The second characteristic was his tunnel vision: he could be totally absorbed in his thoughts and visions for A.A. Many people interpreted this concentration as absent-mindedness, like when he couldn't find his glasses. "Nell, have you seen my glasses?" he would ask. I would answer,

"They're on top of your head, Bill." But I've always been convinced that this trait was important to A.A.'s growth and development. Without Bill's ability to think far ahead into the future, anticipating and envisioning future needs, there might not be an A.A. as we know it today.

In the middle forties, groups were proliferating rapidly at home and were starting abroad. Newspapers, magazines, and especially radio began to discover A.A. in a big way. Radio carried an early kind of soap opera serial called "Aunt Jenny," involving an alcoholic family member, and many cities carried a popular call-in program, "Ask An Alcoholic." Because Bill and Lois traveled so often among the groups in the U.S. and Canada during that decade, the small A.A. office staff had to handle all this publicity. A lot of it came from the box office success of the movie *The Lost Weekend*. Perhaps for the first time an alcoholic was portrayed not as a "Bowery bum" but as a successful, middle-class businessperson who, because of alcohol, was reduced to a "Bowery" level. Because of the public's avid interest in this picture, at least four or five movie companies descended on the office, all within a year or two, seeking our cooperation in making feature films about A.A. An acceptable script by Paramount Pictures was considered for a long time (some of us thought this would be a great idea, since the author was a "Robert Smith"). But, by 1949, Bill and others finally decided against getting involved.

As A.A. was growing, the office was growing, too. By the end of 1949, we had about five A.A. staffers, and about fourteen or more other nonalcoholic employees. Because of Bill's frequent absences from the office, there was sometimes a lack of overall top responsibility. To remedy this, the trustees appointed a general service committee to oversee the office needs and activities on a

8

regular basis. Hank G., chairman of the committee, began to serve as volunteer manager of the office. It later became a salaried position, first part-time and eventually full-time.

I remember Hank as a man of medium height, with a round face and rust-colored hair and moustache. He was an intense man, inclined to be gruff on occasion. But his contributions to the office were many and innovative and he had a profound effect on headquarter's operations. For example, he structured and programmed the 1955 International Convention held in St. Louis. This every fifth-year format is still followed today by G.S.O. Even many outside organizations asked for the set of guidelines he drew up in 1955 for that convention.

Ebby T., the man who first brought the Oxford Group message to Bill, was a familiar visitor at 415 Lexington during the forties. Unfortunately, he never did achieve any lasting sobriety himself. Ebby was a feisty, angry man when drunk and often expressed resentment and jealousy that Bill gave credit to Dr. Bob rather than himself (Ebby) as cofounder. But Bill was unfailingly loyal to Ebby, called him his sponsor, and constantly was concerned about his welfare.

Although accurate membership and group statistics were almost impossible to record (and still are), we estimated there were about 40,000 members in early 1947, in about 1,250 groups. New groups were forming at a rapid rate. It was incredible, by 1950, for us in the office to watch A.A. spread to Australia, Mexico, Ireland, Scotland, England, continental Europe, and South Africa, and a bit later to Alaska, the Pacific Islands, Hawaii, and the Orient. Canada had started in the early forties.

Those early members and groups were often terribly isolated. They had no one to communicate with except our office. We were, in many ways, their only contact or source for help in staying sober. They wrote long letters describing how they felt, how they were doing, what luck they were having in finding other alcoholics, and about the joy, excitement, and achievement of actually getting a group started. Those wonderful letters of that decade are a very important base upon which the present archives rests. No history of the Fellowship can really be complete without sharing the emotion, the problems, and the joys and disappointments of that early time.

As far as carrying the message abroad, no other single individual did more to plant the seed of A.A. in the dozens of countries he visited than Captain Jack S. A native of Maine, Jack had gone to sea as a young man and the sailor's life had led him into alcoholism. Fortunately, he found A.A. and recovered to become captain of an oil tanker. This job gave him a unique opportunity to carry the A.A. message.

Knowing how difficult it was for a lone sailor to stay sober on a ship at sea, Captain Jack organized the "Internationalists" Seamen Group in 1949. These are A.A.s on the high seas who correspond with each other through a designated staff member in the New York office. Captain Jack started this wonderful service by first establishing A.A. contacts in the ports where the ships docked. He visited bars up and down the coasts of Africa and the Far East, leaving copies of the Big Book. The Port Contacts not only gave the A.A. sailors an alternative to the customary drunken sprees, but they were often the core around which an A.A. group developed in a foreign country. Along with Loners, members living in remote locations with no group to attend, the Internationalists and Port Contacts now constitute a whole, loosely formed subgroup within A.A., numbering many hundreds, who correspond with a staff member at G.S.O. and with each other. The G.S.O. also publishes a special bulletin for them, described on the masthead as a "meeting by mail," the distribution of which started in the early fifties.

We were, I think, in perhaps the most turbulent, but most exciting decade (1945–55) in the history of Alcoholics Anonymous. Bill and Lois were caught up in all the activity, too. And of course, so were Dr. Bob and Anne, to the extent their health permitted in the latter part of the forties. (Anne died in 1949; Dr. Bob in 1950.)

As receptionist, I was often the first one to learn from a visitor that a new group had been formed in his or her community or area. I would take the visitor to the records clerk to verify that we had received notification. If not, Yolanda would take the information. Back in the reception room, we would make a little ceremony of placing a colored pin in the proper location on the big U.S. map on the wall. (This big map is now located in Bill's studio, up at Stepping Stones.)

All of us were aware of the growing pains and problems that Alcoholics Anonymous was experiencing in those early decades because our office was always asked to help solve them. Besides Bill and Dr. Bob, there were lots of local "founders" around the country. And these founders did pretty much as they wanted to, making their own rules and regulations. Many were area-newsletter editors, or participants in local radio interviews or programs. Other early members believed that they were the real founders of A.A., and that Bill's role, especially, was exaggerated. This really was a time of trial and error.

Clubhouses for A.A. members were being started in many areas, causing confusion and other problems as to their purpose, management, and relationship to the Fellowship of A.A. I remember a couple of them got raided for illegal gambling.

And the family members and spouses of alcoholics often had their own set of problems. In the early forties, not all A.A. meetings were "open," so spouses began to meet by themselves. On Lois and Bill's trips around the country, Lois paid special attention to the wives' concerns, encouraging them to help themselves, meet together, follow the Steps and so forth. I think lots of people think Al-Anon began in 1951, but Lois had been laying the groundwork long before.

Money was also a problem at both the group and national level. In 1947, when I came on board, Bill found himself caught in the middle on a critical situation involving the National Committee for Education on Alcoholism (N.C.E.A.). Marty M., who founded the committee in 1944 (later to be called the National Council on Alcoholism and now called the National Council on Alcoholism and Drug Dependence) was enthusiastic and persuasive, and was a personal friend of Bill and Dr. Bob. Both Bill and Dr. Bob believed so strongly in what she was trying to accomplish during the forties that they publicly endorsed her organization by allowing both their names to appear on the N.C.E.A. letterhead.

But in 1946, Marty had circulated a solicitation letter for funds, and included the view that A.A. would also certainly benefit by a contribution to the N.C.E.A. cause. This brought a spate of outraged calls and letters from A.A. members and raised such a hullaballoo over a long period of time (about four years) that I seriously feared it might be the end of A.A. right there.

During this period, Bill had been traveling around the country. I think he was on the West Coast when this incident exploded. The trustees called a news conference. They explained A.A.'s tradition of self-support and emphasized that the Fellowship did no soliciting of funds from outside sources. But, as so often happens, some good things did come out of that long, stressful period. Bill and Dr. Bob, acknowledging their error, had their names removed from the letterhead of the N.C.E.A. stationery, thus terminating what could be considered a serious infringement of the Sixth and Seventh Traditions. Also, the experience had an impact on the final wording of the "short form" of the Seventh Tradition, which was accepted, along with the other Traditions, by the entire Fellowship at the 1950 Anniversary Convention in Cleveland.

I look back in awe at the many critically important events that occurred in my first decade at the office. In one single year, 1950, there were many turning points in A.A. history. As he told me that first day, Bill was embroiled in a debate with the trustees regarding their place, and his, in the total A.A. picture and about plans for a structural linkage between service entities and A.A. groups. In the middle forties he wrote many long, well-thought-out memos about a "Code of Tradition," a "Code for Headquarters," and a "Code for the *Grapevine*." He was pushing hard to promote self-government for the Fellowship through a general service conference. Bill also made many visits out among the groups to promote his plans.

In 1950, the First International Convention of A.A. was held in Cleveland, where the Twelve Traditions were accepted and Dr. Bob gave his last talk. Bill and Lois visited A.A. members abroad for the first time. During another trip around the U.S., Bill recognized the need for organizing the many family groups in existence and pressured Lois to undertake this service, which she did, with her friend, Anne B.'s, assistance. Dr. Bob passed away later that year, on November 16. And the headquarters office moved to larger quarters around the corner at 141 East Forty-fourth Street.

Later that same year, in addition to my other duties, I began to work directly with Bill. The secretary who had been taking his dictation resigned, and the demands on Bill had increased so enormously that he needed someone to be secretary, aide, and assistant combined. So Helen B., a senior staff member who had also been helping with his correspondence, recommended me for the job. By now I had come to terms with any plans or thoughts of leaving for Mexico. Bill had often teased me about abandoning them and "heading for the border."

In 1952 Bill decided to combine, in the form of a hardcover book, the Traditions essays he had written for the *Grapevine* in 1946 with a new series of essays on how each of the Steps applied to sober living. I remember a letter he wrote in July of that year to Father Ed Dowling in St. Louis in which he said:

> The problem of the Steps has been to broaden and deepen them, both for newcomers and oldtimers . . . We have to deal with atheists, agnostics, believers, depressives, paranoids, clergymen, psychiatrists, and all and sundry. How to widen the opening so it seems right and reasonable to enter there and at the same time to avoid distractions, distortions, and the certain prejudices of all who may read, seems fairly much of an assignment.

As soon as *Twelve Steps and Twelve Traditions* was published in January 1953, it was an immediate success— somewhat to Bill's surprise. By October, 25,000 copies had been shipped. It has remained A.A.'s second largest selling book.

About this time, 1954, Bill got the idea of forming a

"writing and research team" consisting of the two of us, plus Ed B., the relative of a famous American painter. Ed had had considerable success as a writer and editor before alcoholism ruined his career. He had been recently discharged from Rockland State Hospital and had undergone a laryngectomy. Unable to speak, he communicated by means of well-expressed handwritten or typed notes. The purpose of the team was to turn out several projects Bill had in mind: (1) a second edition of *Alcoholics Anonymous*—at the time, Bill was traveling around, taping personal stories from old-timers, for an updated story section, but he needed help transcribing and editing; (2) the full-length history of Alcoholics Anonymous; but since Bill's depressions precluded this kind of commitment, this ended up as *Alcoholics Anonymous Comes of Age* in 1957—though Bill still hoped to do the full history; and (3) "In All Our Affairs," the working title of a book that would be a summary of how he and others applied the program spiritually and practically; this idea eventually evolved into *The A.A. Way of Life*, later retitled *As Bill Sees It*.

Our writing and research team began working for a short time at 141 East Forty-fourth Street in 1954, but early in the following year we moved to a space in a loft building at 305 East Forty-fifth Street, adjacent to the shipping department, which had also been relocated on the same floor. We moved to relieve the overcrowding at the General Service Office, but even more to get away from interruptions and distractions. We set to work with enthusiasm for about three years and produced the second edition of the Big Book in 1955 and started preparations for *Alcoholics Anonymous Comes of Age*. Although Ed B.'s considerable talents were helpful, he often became frustrated at our sometimes indecisive writing schedule and so was released to look for a steadier job. Tom P., Bill's editor for *Twelve Steps and Twelve Traditions*, later took over as editor for *Alcoholics Anonymous Comes of Age* and guided it through publication. So for most of the years, 1956–60, I was all by myself at 305 East Forty-fifth Street. Bill came down once a week, which was his usual schedule.

For the *Alcoholics Anonymous Comes of Age* project, I dug into the old files and records of the groups and the Alcoholic Foundation office going all the way back to when it started in 1940 down on Vesey Street in lower Manhattan. During the forties these files were stored in a downtown Manhattan warehouse. Now they were in the shipping room right outside our door in boxes towering all the way to the ceiling.

Bill encouraged me to continue the digging and sorting, and to organize this material. He once declared:

> The whole story of A.A. is hidden in these boxes, waiting only to be searched out . . . Thanks to our research activity, it is now certain that the basic facts of A.A.'s growth and development can never be distorted.

This "new undertaking of Nell's," as he called it, was really the beginning of the A.A. Archives.

Some of my most vivid and touching memories of the early office at 415 Lexington centered around our Christmas parties. A.A. was not against drinking, and the staff always made sure that the nonalcoholics were served drinks if they wanted them—as I remember, everybody did. At one Christmas party, some of the younger female employees began flirting through the office windows with some fellows having a party in their office, which happened to be that of a national distiller, across the side street in the Chrysler Building. They were communicating

16

with gestures and handwritten signs, the men inviting our women employees to come over to their party. Things were going great until the men discovered our people were from A.A. and were extending the same invitation.

We would sing carols, play records, dance, and exchange gifts, with Bill acting as Santa. But the high point of every Christmas party was when Bill sat down, in the middle of the room, in the straight-backed chair, tilted it back, and we all sat cross-legged on the floor, around his feet, to hear him tell, once again, how A.A. began. This was what he called the "bedtime story." In closing, he always emphasized the special importance of our own contributions of service, explaining how individually we made a difference in the sobriety and in the lives of innumerable alcoholics and their families everywhere.

This renewed sense of purpose, this unique sense of unity of our small, close-knit family, our special togetherness at this time, are memories I'll cherish forever.

3

BILL W. AT WORK: INFLUENCES AND CONTRIBUTIONS

Watching Bill at work, I was always struck by his amazing foresight. Bill always thought in terms of the Big Picture, the goal ahead. He was willing to try new and even risky methods. He wasn't distracted by the myriad details, squabbles, and tempests in a teapot that characterized early A.A. His eyes were on the future, not on the "niggles and naggles," as he called them. His aim was to push for ideas that would help the Fellowship develop and grow and eventually reach alcoholics worldwide.

"On the anvils of experience," Bill said, "the structure of our society was hammered out." And to this very day the need to preserve A.A.'s experience continues. History, dates, and events are important to record, but the experience gained from those events is something else, to be used to guide us into the future so that past mistakes are not repeated. This is the purpose of an archive: to preserve the experience as well as the "when" and "where" of history.

Instead of becoming mired in the problems and growing pains, Bill took the advice of Earl T., founder of the Chicago group, and codified this experience in the middle forties. He was able to synthesize it into a set of guidelines for the survival, unity, and effectiveness of the Fellowship. Initially, he labeled them "Twelve Points to Assure Our Future." Later they were named the "Twelve Traditions." Had Bill tried to call them rules or regulations, they might never have been accepted.

As it was, however, it was pretty tough trying to sell them to the groups. They weren't ready to listen, a condition that came as no surprise to Bill, I'm sure. As he often said, the groups were interested and eager to have him share his own story and A.A. beginnings, but not to listen to any more "discussion about those damned traditions." So, again at the urging of Earl T. in 1949, Bill reduced them into a "short form" and they were accepted at the convention in 1950.

Another significant contribution by Bill was how he learned to communicate his own recovery "to share his experience, strength, and hope," as A.A. puts it—with other alcoholics. Bill loved to talk. His hold on audiences was almost hypnotic. At one of the New York annual "Bill's Birthday Dinners" in the sixties, I was sitting with Herb M., the General Service Office general manager. Herb could be critical of some of Bill's ideas, or the timing of them, anyway, and often argued with him. So on this night I was touched to see Herb drying his eyes and blowing his nose along with all the other A.A.s in the audience as Bill finished speaking. He reached everybody he talked to.

Bill was a great synthesizer. In his writings, his talks, and his vision of A.A., he put together ideas from widely disparate sources. From the Oxford Group, he took "Self-Surrender," "Conversion," "Honesty," "Restoration,"

"Witnessing," "Sharing," and "Daily Practice," all of which became the basis for Steps Three through Twelve. The essential principle of A.A., a fellowship meeting to share the common experience of positive change, came directly from the Oxford Group. And the summer he and Dr. Bob spent together in Akron, working out ways to apply Oxford Group principles specifically to alcoholics, formed the basis for his later contributions to the program.

From William James' *Varieties of Religious Experience* Bill derived the idea of deflation of the ego or "reaching a bottom" as a prerequisite to accepting a Power greater than oneself. This, and the spiritual experience he had himself, were articulated as the First Step and formed the basis for recovery.

Bill admired James greatly. Both were eager to explore the spiritual, the nature of God, and psychic phenomena. Later, in July 1965, an article called "William James and Alcoholics Anonymous" appeared in the magazine *America*. Written by Fr. Robert J. Roth, S.J., then associate professor of philosophy at Fordham University, the article was based on the discussions and sharing at the 30th Anniversary Convention of Alcoholics Anonymous at Toronto, Canada, in 1965. Any A.A. member or friend of the Fellowship reading this article could easily recognize the identifying characteristics, the philosophic and spiritual identities these two New Englanders shared. It is a fascinating and revealing article. (This article was also reprinted in the *Grapevine* in August 1967.)

From de Tocqueville's *Democracy in America*, Bill developed ideas for the structure of A.A. that helped save it from the self-destruction of many other organizations. Bill described these ideas in a 1956 letter to J.J. Hennessy, S.J.:

At the group level, in the sense of association with each other, we have what is really an anarchy—a pretty benign one, of course. When the group begins to function however, then the majority vote rules and we have a pure democracy. When we reach the level of the General Service Conference, we find a democracy which includes some republican principles. And the original hierarchy, the Board of Trustees, is still there but now made completely responsible to an electorate. Then, too we have a dictatorship —and how! God constantly says to us, 'I trust you will find and do my will.' John Barleycorn, always at our elbow, says, 'If you don't conform, I'll kill you or drive you mad.' So we have all the advantages and more, of the modern dictatorship.

Another book that Bill valued was *This Believing World* by Lewis Browne—something I well understand because this book helped along my own spiritual awakening. Jim B., before going to Philadelphia to help start the group there, was one of the early members in New York and he wrote in his own unpublished story of A.A.'s beginnings:

From this book of comparative religion, I believe Bill attained a remarkable perception of possible future pitfalls for groups of our kind, for it clearly shows that the major failures of religions and cults in the past have been due to three things: too much organization, politics, money or power.

Dr. William Silkworth, "the little doctor who loved drunks," who defined alcoholism as an obsession and allergy, an illness of the whole man, of body, mind, and spirit, deeply influenced Bill. His holistic approach to physical and mental disorders was adopted by A.A. and so influenced attitudes in the fields of medicine and social sciences that today other diseases are treated as illnesses of the whole person.

Bill was responsible for A.A.'s structural characteristics such as corporate poverty, lack of personal authority ("our leaders are but trusted servants"), and having the least organization possible to carry the message. Many members thought that these ideas would never work, but of course they do. After Bill's death, Lois and I talked about their sources. She believed that St. Francis of Assisi (who Bill deeply admired) influenced Bill's thinking, particularly the corporate poverty idea. Lois wasn't sure just when Bill became interested in St. Francis—it was certainly in the early forties, probably through Father Ed Dowling, S.J., or Sister Francis.

A devoted and enthusiastic friend of A.A., Bill, and Lois, Sister Francis owned and operated Joy Farm in Kent, Connecticut, which early A.A.s in New York and Connecticut took over from her as a drying-out place in 1940 and renamed it High Watch Farm.

Bill told the story this way:

> Up in the hills of Connecticut (near Kent) . . . a group of farms belonged to a dear lady known affectionately to countless A.A.s as Sister Francis. This wonderfully good soul, out of her own pocket, had operated these farms for charity—for the aged, for children and for any wayfarer who passed by.[1]

Sister Francis called it the Ministry of the High Watch, and she apparently had special compassion for the alcoholics who sought help there. "In the summer of 1939," Bill related, "Marty M. . . . conducted a party of us to Connecticut, where we met Sister Francis"[2] and to see the

200-acre farm that remained after Sister Francis had to sell off the rest of her property.

Marty M. recalled later that after she and Bill had admired the serene beauty of the setting in the Berkshires, they found themselves in a room that served as a chapel in the pre-revolutionary colonial farmhouse. They were overwhelmed with the almost palpable spiritual presence around them. Bill turned and murmured softly, "God, Marty, you can almost cut it with a knife!"

According to Bill, "Sister Francis seemed to be as delighted with us as we were with her. She offered us full use of the place if some of us would create a board of trustees to look after it."[3] The rest farm that came into being as a result of Sister Francis' gift is a charming place. It is a wonderful spot to send anyone who needs extra time to recuperate after hospitalization. High Watch Farm has operated ever since 1940 on a simple program of immersion in the Twelve Steps and other principles of Alcoholics Anonymous.

In the office Bill and I shared hung a rather good oil portrait of him painted by a member in the Midwest. When I cleared out the office after Bill's death, I took the painting home for safekeeping. I finally decided to give it to High Watch. I think it still hangs today on a wall of one of the rooms where they have the daily spiritual meetings so important to the recovery process.

Likewise, Sister M. Victorine, a contemporary of Sister Ignatia's from A.A.'s early days in Ohio, was involved with Charity Hospital in Cleveland and touched the lives of many alcoholics in those days. Al G., an early Cleveland member, said in *Doctor Bob and the Good Oldtimers* that "St. Vincent's Charity Hospital, later to become the home of Rosary Hall, followed Deaconess in 1940 by taking in patients in single rooms, and essentially Sister Victorine

24

established a ward there."[4] Ed A., a very early Ohio member, remained a close and caring friend to her right up to her death in January 1988.

Bill was also influenced by reading about Mary Baker Eddy, the Christian Science founder, particularly about the dangers of single-person leadership. Her early teacher and mentor had decried Eddy's failure to give him proper credit for the critical ideas she later adopted as integral parts of her teaching, resulting in a lot of controversy. A 1943 letter from Bill to a friend alludes to this incident:

> No one in A.A. should ever be subjected to such
> temptations . . . A.A. should always give full
> credit to its several well-springs of inspiration
> and should always consider these people among
> the founders of our well-loved society.

Bill himself certainly set an example in giving credit to others. And he followed his own advice, acknowledging almost from the beginning Dr. Bob as cofounder, crediting the Oxford Group and its New York leader, Dr. Sam Shoemaker, as a source of ideas, and citing James' *Varieties of Religious Experience* as a source of inspiration. Dr. Silkworth was asked to contribute "The Doctor's Opinion" to the Big Book. No one knew better than Bill himself that "nobody invented A.A." "Everything in A.A. is borrowed from somewhere else," he often stated.

The evolution of a corporate structure for providing and linking A.A. services can be credited to Bill's persuasion and persistence. The trustees were receptive to overall responsibility but they conceived of their responsibility as primarily custodial; they were not an "action" body. They were at first wary of the idea of the conference and later of the established conference itself. In the early years, delegates were new on the job, and although they understood their responsibility for the whole operation they were

25

somewhat in awe of the trustees, many of them having had no direct connection to the office. The A.A. staff members at the office functioned pretty much on their own and in the forties weren't sure of their own role in the whole picture. The *Grapevine* office was off by itself in that era, not yet part of the final structure either.

Bill foresaw that this lack of linkage of services and lack of direct cooperation could lead to internal conflict and contained the seeds of possible destruction of Alcoholics Anonymous. Having pushed through the conference idea, with the "final responsibility and ultimate authority" in the hands of the groups, Bill then tried to pull together all these separate elements into what he termed the "Third Legacy of Service" (the first two Legacies being Recovery and Unity, through the Twelve Steps and the Twelve Traditions, respectively).

He put together the *Third Legacy Manual*, later renamed *The A.A. Service Manual*. It explains simply and clearly how the whole structure works. This manual, however, was essentially a nuts-and-bolts guide. Therefore, in 1959, he began to write a supplement to the manual: "to record the 'why' of our service structure in such a fashion that the highly valuable experience of the past, and the lessons we have drawn from that experience, can never be forgotten or lost."[5]

To this day, not much is known about the writing of *Twelve Concepts for World Service*, as he called this booklet. Probably more than any other of his books, this represents how he thought. In 1959, he wrote out the entire manuscript in longhand, painfully working it over, deleting, inserting, and changing as he went. Then he passed it for me to type up—and retype—several editings, as usual. It was finally approved by the conference in 1962 and published.

When they were introduced, the Twelve Concepts were greeted with indifference—followed by years of virtual neglect. After all, they applied mainly to those involved in service, and were extremely tough reading. I seem to recall that the A.A. staff at the office was given a study course in the Concepts prior to one of the conferences. However, there has been a renaissance of interest over the last decade or two—perhaps helped along by former staff member Eve M.'s excellent presentation of them in her visits to groups. I believe that they—and the structure they describe—are one of Bill's greatest contributions.

Another of Bill's contributions—a major one—is his books. These are the cornerstones of A.A. literature: the Big Book, (*Alcoholics Anonymous*), *Twelve Steps and Twelve Traditions*, and *Alcoholics Anonymous Comes of Age* (which could be described as a vast canvas on which Bill paints a panorama of everything that had happened in A.A. from its birth until the St. Louis Convention, and a portrait of A.A.'s place in the world in 1955). *Twelve Concepts for World Service* is a comprehensive description of authority, responsibility, and leadership in A.A. and the interrelationship of the groups, the trustees, the conference, the G.S.O., and the A.A. Grapevine, Inc. Bill's last book, *As Bill Sees It*, is a collection of quotations and excerpts from the above literature, plus his *Grapevine* articles and letters. By the late sixties, Bill's emphysema was curtailing his activities. Janet G. was a tremendous help in researching my archives files and putting the book together, with Bill's overall input and editing.

In 1988, the A.A. Grapevine, Inc. published *The Language of the Heart*, a 400-page volume of all of Bill's writings that had appeared in their pages since 1944. It's a marvelous work that reveals much about Bill's own growth spiritually and his insight over the years. I think it presents what Bill expected from his long-anticipated final book "In All Our Affairs," the summing-up experience he was unable to undertake due to his deteriorating health.

In light of the vast number of self-help movements that have evolved over the last decade, Bill's openness to sharing A.A. principles, A.A.'s Twelve Steps, and A.A.'s experience with scores of other Twelve Step fellowships must be regarded as one of his most far-reaching contributions. The total membership in such self-help groups is estimated to be in the millions. And it all started with Alcoholics Anonymous and the Fellowship's willingness to share its program with anyone who would be helped. These groups include, among many others, Narcotics Anonymous, Overeaters Anonymous, Gamblers Anonymous, Sexaholics Anonymous, Debtors Anonymous, Incest Survivors Anonymous, etc. After all, Bill said, everything in A.A. is borrowed from somewhere else, so why shouldn't we be willing to share it with others?

However, I think it's important to note that Bill, like the earlier members, did not approve of multi-purpose groups or of drug addicts without alcoholic problems participating as members in closed A.A. meetings. Open meetings, of course, are where all are welcome. The important qualification for membership in A.A. was and is that alcohol must be a major or first problem. Bill spelled it out clearly in at least two *Grapevine* articles: "Who is a Member of Alcoholics Anonymous" (August 1946) and "Problems Other Than Alcohol" (February 1958).

For my part, however, Bill W.'s greatest spiritual contribution of all was his willingness—even eagerness—to step down as leader. From the very first time I met him when I came to work, until his death, he devoted a large part of his energy and time to trying to divest himself of power and authority, instead of trying to hang onto them. This idea was an integral part of the Twelve Traditions. Tradition Two states:

> For our group purpose, there is but one ultimate authority—a loving God as He may express Himself in our group conscience. Our leaders are but trusted servants, they do not govern.

The General Service Conference grew out of this same idea, and Bill had to struggle long and hard to educate the groups to accept this responsibility and authority.

The willingness to step down is even more remarkable, since it seemed to many members contrary to Bill's nature. And in this regard I think he was unique. Most leaders hang on until they either die or are forcibly unseated. But Bill stepped down. Dr. Jack Norris summed it up in his eulogy: "He was willing to let go before we were willing to let go of him."

4

BILL AND LOIS AT HOME

In 1954, I began going up to Stepping Stones an average of every second or third weekend because Bill preferred to work there. Stepping Stones in time became my second home, and Bill and Lois, my family.

Once I returned to New York from visiting friends, stunned by the sudden death of the long-time friend I was about to marry. Bill and Lois drove down from Bedford Hills to pick me up and take me back to Stepping Stones where, for many days, they comforted me as best they could. Another time, I was caught by a sudden appendicitis attack and rushed to the hospital. Bill dashed down to make sure I was okay, and after the operation and recovery period took me back to Stepping Stones for recuperation.

They had no children. Lois had suffered three ectopic pregnancies with accompanying surgery, and they were unable to adopt because of Bill's alcoholism in those days.

Life at Stepping Stones always followed a comfortable, domestic pattern. They shared an early morning "quiet time," a custom retained from their Oxford Group experience. Lois was an avid reader on a variety of subjects, particularly science, art, and archeology. She enjoyed reading aloud to Bill during their quiet time and he enjoyed listening. They also included a prayer and a short period of silent meditation, after which Bill would go downstairs, make coffee, and return with it to their bedroom. Then they would have breakfast and get to work.

Around the house, Bill dressed very casually. He preferred country-style plaid shirts, a jacket, boots, and khaki pants. Outside, he liked to wear a baseball or railroad worker's cap, usually khaki-colored too. I remember one time Bill and Lois were due at the airport, when they were leaving on a trip to the Caribbean. I was there as usual to bid them good-bye and to receive any last-minute instructions regarding the house. As they approached, I was suddenly shocked to see how really casual they looked. Bill was wearing his loose slacks, a plaid woolen shirt, an old jacket with sleeves way too short, and of course, the khaki cap on his head. Lois didn't look any more stylish. She carried a huge shopping bag, containing, I imagine, their manuscripts to edit and correspondence to answer. Those trips were not all travelogues, I found out. Heavy work was done by each of them. I always thought of those trips as extended hideaways: same purpose, just farther away.

But both Bill and Lois did have a good sense of style at their offices, or at meetings and events. They were always very well-dressed. I remember years ago asking Bill what he would like for Christmas. This particular year, he suggested that he could use another pair of slacks. So we went to Abercrombie & Fitch at Bill's suggestion and my apprehension! Bill picked out a nice pair of pants, and I was pleased to make them his Christmas present.

On my weekends at Bedford Hills, more often than not, we would work upstairs. Lois worked on Al-Anon business at her desk, and Bill dictated to me. Or if he was through dictating, he might nap on the couch while I was typing or filing. Other times, Bill and I would be at the same routine in the studio up the hill, while Lois tended to the seasonal needs of the property, especially her beloved garden.

Lois loved gardening. She planned the landscaping— the flower gardens, vegetable garden, shrubs, and even the trees. Early on, she brought from Vermont a number of small evergreens and white birches that are now huge, graceful, and tall. She loved weeding. I can still see her on her hands and knees with a spade, pail, and small stool nearby. Or, each spring, wearing a large, wide-brimmed hat covered with a voluminous white netting, spraying the young fruit trees and flowering trees. A friend, knowing her passion for gardening, once gave her a plaque that she hung on a bedroom wall. It says, "Old gardeners never die; they just lose their bloomers." She loved it.

I will never forget Lois' graciousness as a hostess. In Brooklyn, she had been raised in a household with a small staff of servants. Her life, as she described it, reminded me of how I imagined the English aristocracy lived. And throughout the time I knew her, she maintained the traditions of formality, courtesy, and graciousness she had learned there. For example, at the midday meal at Bedford Hills, which was usually candle-lit and formal, we were served by the cook or whoever was on duty in the kitchen at that time.

It was taboo to call out to the cook, even though the kitchen was only a step or two away. Initially I would try to get the cook's attention unobtrusively, thinking I was being helpful when we needed a missing spoon or a sugar substitute. Lois would reprimand me quickly and would ring a small bell near her plate to let our needs be known.

She also rang it when it was time for the table to be cleared. Lois' insistence on correct manners was very typical of her and something I always admired.

On Friday evenings, Bill would pick me up at the railroad station at Bedford Hills, and Lois would be working in the kitchen, busily preparing the evening meal. While cooking wasn't one of her favorite activities, which she freely admitted, she was an excellent steak-and-potatoes cook. Her pot roasts were a favorite. Waiting for dinner, Bill would always turn to me and say, "Well, Nell, how about some of the old chestnuts?" So, I would sit down at the piano, he would pick up his violin or cello, and we would sail right into favorites like "Home Sweet Home," "In the Gloamin'," or "It's a Long Way to Tipperary" from his war years. "The Wearing of the Green" was a favorite, and he included "Seeing Nellie Home" when I was there.

On Saturdays, when our work was through, we usually took a walk or went for a drive in the late afternoon. Bill would say to Lois, "Daddles, I'll drive," to which Lois would reply, "No, Bill, I'll drive." So they would go back and forth like that and she usually prevailed. Meanwhile, I would make myself comfortable in the back seat. On these long walks and longer car rides, I got to know that beautiful, wooded Westchester countryside in all seasons. Sometimes, we might splurge and eat dinner at one of their favorite area restaurants.

Music was an important part of leisure time at Stepping Stones. Both Bill and Lois liked classical music as I did and kept the radio tuned most of the time to WQXR, our favorite classical music station in New York. I had taken piano lessons back in Kendall, and play tolerably well, but not as well as Lois. Bill taught himself to play first violin in the high school orchestra, which performed for school dances. He belittled this accomplishment by saying, "I

34

was a very bad first violin in a very poor orchestra." Nevertheless, music continued to provide him with a satisfying outlet throughout his life. He once took his violin to Akron on a visit to Dr. Bob and Anne. The story goes that they loved seeing Bill, but could have tolerated a bit less of the violin. For years at the annual Al-Anon picnics at Stepping Stones, he strolled around the grounds, playing like a roving gypsy. Actually, he was better on the cello. He loved to listen to radio performances by Pablo Casals.

Bill owned two violins, the second one a gift from a pioneer member in Milwaukee named Gib K. At the invitation of members in that area, Bill and Lois visited there the year after I came to the office. Gib was in the hospital, terminally ill with cancer when Bill called on him. Gib pressed him to accept a violin he made especially for Bill. Bill treasured this gift all the rest of his life.

Besides playing these instruments, Bill was constantly tinkering with them, taking them apart and putting them together again. I think this was his engineering side taking over. At Stepping Stones, I had the downstairs bedroom, a step up and just beyond the living room. I remember being kept awake past midnight more than once while Bill tinkered with the older, family violin in the living room, sawing away on the strings as he made adjustments. Finally, it wouldn't stand any more improvement and refused to sound its A.

The piano, violin, and cello can still be seen in the corner of the living room at Stepping Stones.

Speaking of tinkering as an example of Bill's engineering bent, I love a story Lois used to tell. In every season except summer, Bill got up before dawn and went downstairs to the cellar to turn on the furnace. It was good to have some warm air circulating in their bedroom for their quiet time and meditation. There was a time in the forties

35

when Bill's sister Helen came to live with them for a few years before she married and moved out west. Bill thought of passing along the furnace starting procedure to Helen, since her bed was located off the living room and directly over the furnace in the cellar. It had occurred to Bill that if he cut a hole in the bedroom floor and attached a long handle to the furnace starter going up through the hole, it would arrive exactly by the side of Helen's bed. Then Helen could wake up early, pull the handle, and start the furnace going, thus eliminating any need for Bill to wake up.

Over the years, Lois reminisced about her family, her childhood, and her young womanhood in Brooklyn and Vermont. Sometimes she would bring out photographs of her family and household and identify the scenes and the people. In fact, she had brought from the Burnham home the forerunner of the first motion-picture machine, an oak box with a crank on the side, called a *Multiscope*. (It still sits on a desk upstairs at Stepping Stones.) Her family acted out some scenes that were photographed in rapid sequence to catch the motion. Viewed through a window in the multiscope box, it looked like a crude motion picture. A unique treasure, indeed, and one which still fascinates visitors to Stepping Stones. I like to show them how it works, turning the crank while they look in.

Bill and Lois got away from the telephone and interruptions a couple times a week, usually by renting a "hideaway," their name for a small, one-room cabin, which area families rented out for certain periods of the year. This enabled them to give full attention to the work at hand; that is, Lois could focus on her writing for Al-Anon and Bill on his current project—whether a book, a memo to the trustees, or (I hopefully anticipated) bringing his accumulated pile of correspondence up to date.

They also enjoyed taking longer trips a couple of times a year. During the spring, they discussed what areas of the states or Canada they would like to visit. I remember how much they enjoyed a trip to Michigan's Upper Peninsula, taking a boat over to Isle Royale to get a close look at the moose (which the wolves were rapidly decimating) and other animals. At one time or another I think they toured just about every state, plus the provinces of Canada. (Lois describes these trips in her autobiography, *Lois Remembers*.) Also, during the fall or winter, usually during the holiday season, they would visit places outside the U.S. and Canada. It was always exciting to get letters and reviews of these places: Mexico (with Dr. Emily—Bill's mother—joining them from San Diego), the Yucatan Peninsula, the Isles of Scilly (off the coast of Cornwall, England, a place Bill had always wanted to visit), the Canary Islands, the Caribbean Islands, Panama, and many other locations.

During their absence, I would take the train up to Bedford Hills to check on the house and grounds, and to look over the mail, which Harriet, their cook-housekeeper, would bring in daily. If some letters needed immediate replies, I would type them out on the typewriter upstairs, or take them back to the New York office. After each visit, I'd write Bill and Lois, keeping them up to date on Stepping Stones matters—the mail, events, whatever I thought they should know about. Usually Bill would have things he wanted to check out, and they would both send me letters, sharing the interesting highlights of each trip and places they'd visited. I have a good-sized folder of these letters.

Bill and Lois were also great walkers. When they first moved to Bedford Hills in 1941, they were practically the only people in the area, so they created their own walking trails. As time passed, more and more people settled there. Even when the area became more populated, Bill and Lois managed to keep portions of their original trails, which by then wound through well-tended lawns, side yards, or under the kitchen windows of new neighbors. As Bill was a familiar sight, people would hail him from their porches or kitchens and he would stop to chat with them.

His walking was a lifeline for him in those years of his sometimes crippling depressions. On days when he could scarcely get out of bed, he would force himself to walk, taking deep breaths. Today, I read articles by doctors recommending this as one of the best possible therapies for maintaining good physical and mental health, especially in combating depression.

Lois was almost as dedicated a walker herself. She and I kept up the walks for many years after Bill died. Lois was especially fond of the spring season, when we would inventory the winter's damage to the property: the broken branches and wild undergrowth that needed to be cleared. This was always more Lois' concern than Bill's. Bill took charge of the larger needs, building the garage and studio for example, but was so preoccupied with A.A.'s needs and problems that he just didn't give the attention to it that Lois did.

In the spring, Lois especially loved viewing the first baby leaves of the trees and bushes—the pink and white buds of the magnolias and dogwoods, for example. This was always a spiritual adventure for me when, on those chilly days in late March, we would walk all around the property and observe, always with the same sense of awe, the annual, mysterious unfolding of the fresh, young season.

With equal anticipation, she awaited the spring arrival of the bluebirds (her favorite, but unaccountably absent in recent years), robins, towhees, doves, scarlet tanagers, thrushes, and the just-passing-through grosbeaks. There are many bird feeders located around Stepping Stones. The one hanging outside the window of Bill and Lois' upstairs bedroom was a special source of joy for Lois in her later years. Often confined to her bed, she would watch with great amusement the aggressive behavior of the purple finches, chickadees, sparrows, cardinals, and others as they flocked around the feeder, jumping from one perch to another, often driving off other birds. She was particularly tickled when one of them would cock its head and peer inquisitively through the window at her.

In the fall, Lois and I would savor the beauty of the autumn colors. We would always pick huge white and purple hydrangeas for the house, and some for me to take back to my New York apartment.

I recall one episode in the spring of 1970 that moves me deeply even as I write about it today. Bill's health had deteriorated by this time, and this was one of his few good walking days outside. The three of us, starting on a walk, decided to try out a new, hilly road. At one point, Lois and I stopped to examine an unfamiliar species of flower. As Lois was telling me about it, I turned to see Bill walking on ahead of us, trudging along the upgrade, hands clasped behind his back, leaning forward as he always did. As his figure became smaller and smaller in the distance, I experienced a sudden but not unexpected premonition that this was to be the last walk the three of us would take together, which it was. Bill was literally and symbolically moving ahead of us on his own while Lois and I lingered with the beauties of this world. A moment later, Bill moved out of our sight.

5

THE PERSONAL BILL

During my 23 years of observing Bill at home at Stepping Stones and at work in the office, I came to appreciate his humanity. I saw him counsel innumerable people at home as well as in the office. He was always a sympathetic listener in these circumstances, a true counselor to A.A. friends and others, not only with their alcoholic problems but with their personal concerns. Bill always gave them pragmatic answers, not lofty, theoretical opinions. Bill was compassionate, understanding, and caring.

I remember an article in an early *Grapevine*, the February 1946 issue, called "From the Outside Looking In," written by Jessica Bové, a nonalcoholic secretary to a New York member. Her boss suggested that she attend an A.A. meeting to learn something about the Fellowship. He suggested one of the monthly meetings because a number of A.A.s, as well as nonalcoholics, would be sharing, giving an overall view of A.A. She said she would be happy to go, and after the meeting she wrote a perceptive and affecting article. Besides commenting on her boss' contribution to the occasion, she said:

I should have realized before any time had

passed . . . that here is a way of life which *anyone* can practice . . . it does not take an A.A. to practice the principles of the A.A. program . . .[6]

And:

I have yet to meet a friendlier, more practical, or easier-to-know God than I met at the A.A. meeting . . .[7]

Among many other observations, she commented on Bill's talk:

I'm not at all surprised to find that he is one of the founders of A.A. I think a fellow who needed a friendly hand, and wise counsel, whether he suffered from alcoholism or not, could be sure of a truly sympathetic understanding and the right answer, if he just asked Bill about it . . .[8]

Bill was articulate. I often wondered where he got it— probably not from his education, which was in engineering and science. In his talks, he had a natural eloquence, and in his writings, he had the gift of finding the word that expressed exactly what he wanted to convey. He was not necessarily erudite, but his choice of language was apt and to the point. When we were working on articles, book chapters, or letters that might be "for the record," they usually went through several drafts, each heavily edited by Bill. Tom P., a friend and superb writer and speaker himself, openly admired this quality in Bill's work. Even though Bill asked Tom to edit some of his manuscripts before publication—specifically *Twelve Steps and Twelve Traditions* and *Alcoholics Anonymous Comes of Age*— Tom seldom changed Bill's words, concentrating instead on the flow of the thought, sentence structure, and paragraphing.

Bill had a wonderful sense of humor. He was a story-teller. But he was not much interested in current jokes making the rounds. On many occasions, I watched as friends attempted to share jokes of this kind with him. When the friend delivered the punch line, Bill would usually just stare at him without reacting in any way.

Bill loved to tell Vermont stories in authentic dialect. He didn't have a noticeable regional accent in his normal speech—unlike Dr. Bob, who was unmistakably a Vermonter. Regaling us with these stories or relating drunken episodes of his own or others, he would not just amuse us, he would send us into gales of laughter.

One of the more serious and touching stories Bill loved to share concerned his boyhood friend, Mark Whalon. The story goes that one day, in walking through a large, wooded area, Mark spied a small abandoned cabin among the trees and decided to investigate it by looking through a window. He then decided to try the door, which opened promptly. Hanging on one of the walls was a picture of a good-looking lady, who appealed to Mark right away. He must have taken the picture away with him for he discovered after investigation that the picture was that of a well-known stage and screen actress, Constance Cummings. Soon after this, he learned that the actress was to appear in a Broadway play in New York. So he wrote her a letter, explaining how he came to see her picture in an abandoned cabin in the Vermont woods. This must have intrigued her, for she wrote him and invited him to town to meet her, which he did. They remained good friends, meeting whenever she was in the city, until Mark died in 1956.

Once at the office, about the time I came to work there, Bill couldn't find a certain document and accused Marion, our office manager, of losing it. She indignantly denied it, but Bill kept nagging. Finally, he found the paper in a drawer in his own desk. In embarrassment, he dropped down on all fours and crawled out to Marion's desk with the document in his teeth, begging her forgiveness.

In this instance he was mocking himself, but he possessed genuine humility. He was unfailingly self-deprecatory. Underneath, he had a healthy ego, but he kept it pretty well reined in. Perhaps his efforts to push off credit to other people were one way of doing this. His constant, insistent efforts to relinquish his own authority as a founder-leader were further evidence of his humility.

In the early 1960s, following the appearance of a critical appraisal of A.A. in articles by Arthur Cain in *Harper's* magazine and the *Saturday Evening Post*, Bill wrote a piece for a 1963 *Grapevine* entitled, "Our Critics Can Be Our Benefactors." He was open to criticism and listened keenly to what others were saying.

I personally think that people's perceptions of Bill's ego in the early days arose from his continuous and persistent efforts to convince the trustees and members to support the structure and vision he had for the Fellowship. This perception was not helped by the fact that Bill himself talked about his ego and his power-driving tendencies. I feel he magnified these tendencies some of the time, perhaps to make people feel he was "one of the boys."

I've listened many times as Bill explained his own view of humility, similar to the early Greek "Middle Way" philosophy. As Bill expressed it, we need to follow a middle road, to strike a balance—neither wearing the Uriah Heep cloak of false humility, which he called "force-feeding of humble pie," nor straying into material achievements and admiration of one's own importance. Bill's definition of humility was willingness to seek God's will in your life and then follow it. I'm reminded of a statement I saw once posted on the bulletin board of an alcoholic rehabilitation facility. It read: "There is but one God, and today you are not him." That's pretty close to Bill's view of humility.

I suppose, over the years, more outsiders have questioned me about anonymity than about anything else in A.A. And certainly it was the question most frequently directed to Bill.

In A.A.'s infancy, the main value of anonymity was to ensure protection of the newcomer. As Bill once explained, "Because of the stigma of alcoholism, most alcoholics wanted to be anonymous." When the earliest members emerged bravely from the protective mantle of the Oxford Group, they sought another protective mantle, namely that of being anonymous.

There were other reasons for anonymity in the early days of the Fellowship. What if an alcoholic who had openly proclaimed his membership went out and got drunk in public? That would destroy confidence in the new movement. And, practically speaking, there was the fear of being overwhelmed by more pleas for help and requests for information than they could possibly handle. Soon it was realized that the mantle of anonymity fostered and preserved the one-to-one peer relationship between well-known members and those "newly arrived" at group meetings.

As the membership grew and anonymity breaks increased in the late forties, it dawned on A.A. that anonymity served a much deeper spiritual purpose. It prevented the egos of the members from driving them to run after money, fame, and power at A.A.'s expense. It fostered personal sacrifice for the benefit of A.A. rather than self, and it came to be described as the firm base upon which A.A. stands.

Even Bill himself went through this metamorphosis. He once wrote to a friend who was questioning the value of anonymity:

> Just before publication of the (Big) Book, I toyed with the idea of signing my name to it. I even thought of calling A.A. "the Wilson movement." Had I then dropped my anonymity, it is entirely possible that you and thousands of others might not be alive today. This movement would have gotten off to a false start entirely.

In January 1946, Bill wrote:

> The word "anonymity" has for us an immense spiritual significance . . . subtly but powerfully it reminds us . . . that we have renounced personal glorification in public; that our movement not only preaches but actually practices a truly humble modesty . . .[9] In a spiritual sense, anonymity amounts to the renunciation of personal prestige . . .[10]

In recent years a rash of film stars, sports figures, authors, and others have broken their anonymity at the public level. There is nothing new about this. Rollie H., a famous baseball player, was one of the first to go public back in 1939 (though a sports reporter was really responsible), followed in the forties by Lillian R., a popular singer; a well-known radio announcer; and "Happiness Joe," a New York radio late-night host, who I think was Lillian's first contact with A.A. Obviously there was a positive side to their speaking out about their membership. Many prospects first heard of A.A. through the resulting publicity, and when Lillian R. traveled to Australia as an entertainer, she gave the small A.A. effort there an enormous boost. But, sad to say, Lillian eventually went back to drinking. Bill, speaking of such instances, used one of his favorite expressions. "The good is often the enemy of the best."

But it was also felt that there is such a thing as being too anonymous. Most members are known to each other only by their first names, but those who, through misunderstanding or just plain preference, withhold their identity completely even at the private level, may be denying help to the suffering alcoholic who needs it. After all, there has to be a means of reaching each other.

Bill felt very strongly about anonymity. He spoke about it at every opportunity right up until and including what A.A. members know as "Bill's Last Message" in the fall of 1970, just before his death. He best summed up his views, I think, at the St. Louis Convention in 1955, when he said:

> The entire future of our fellowship hangs upon this principle. If we continue to be filled with the spirit and practice of anonymity, no shoal or reef can wreck us. If we forget this principle, the lid to Pandora's box will be off and the spirits of Money, Power and Prestige will be loosed among us . . . No A.A. principle merits more study and application than this one. I am positive that A.A.'s anonymity is the key to longtime survival.

This was the example that Bill set in his own life regarding anonymity. Though he would doubtless have enjoyed receiving some of the honors offered to him during the years of his stewardship, he declined them all. Even in those rare instances when he did venture cautiously into public situations (as, for example, at the Harold Hughes Senate Hearings on alcoholism in the late sixties), he made sure his anonymity would be respected and protected at the public level. Bill personally declined or directed to A.A. many awards including: awards and recognitions from colleges (given to A.A.); the Lasker Award (given to A.A. itself); an honorary doctorate from Yale University; a Time magazine cover story; and a post-humous honorary degree from Norwich University, his alma mater in Vermont (declined by Lois on his behalf).

I think Bill was essentially nonreligious, although he was deeply spiritual. His whole life was changed by a profound spiritual experience, which he has described in detail. The Oxford Group Fellowship, which was responsible for Bill's early sobriety, was often regarded by outsiders as a religious movement, though their concept of a "Higher Power" left a lot of latitude for personal interpretation. I have already mentioned Bill's affection for and reliance on his "spiritual sponsor," Father Ed Dowling. And about the time I came to the office, Bill was or just had been, taking instruction in the Roman Catholic faith regularly with Monsignor Fulton Sheen. His sessions with Fulton Sheen contained a lot of argument on both sides, I heard, and so the instruction didn't last long. He never did convert to Catholicism; Lois told me that he really hadn't intended to. But he was pleased when disillusioned and disbelieving alcoholics, as a result of recovering in A.A., returned to active church affiliation.

And yet, for all this deep interest in varieties of spiritual beliefs, Bill was not a churchgoer and avoided joining any particular denomination. By way of explanation, he wrote in *Alcoholics Anonymous Comes of Age*: "Dr. Bob held certain religious convictions, and so do I . . . Nothing, however, could be so unfortunate for A.A.'s future as an attempt to incorporate any of our personal theological views into A.A. teaching, practice, or tradition."[11]

That was probably part of his motive, but from my own discussions with him, I believe it was deeper than that. He

48

was open to all spiritual thinking and did not want to confine himself to one interpretation or creed. As Bill expressed more than once, he "shopped the pie counter" of religion and philosophy.

In his politics, Bill was a rock-ribbed, Vermont conservative. I am a liberal. We argued a lot at election time. Finally, I got weary of arguing and listening to him expound his political views. Like most people on this subject, he was stubborn and wouldn't yield an inch. In his drinking days, he had written fiery letters to President Roosevelt, letters Lois kept "for the record." In the fifties, he felt that Adlai Stevenson, the Democratic candidate for President (and my favorite), was almost a traitor because he suggested that nuclear testing in the Pacific should be curtailed, an action which was taken not too long afterward.

One night Adlai was speaking on television. Every time he made a statement Bill didn't agree with, which was most of them, Bill would frown and glance over at me disapprovingly—as if I were responsible. When Lois had had enough of this, she went to bed. I stayed up. At the breakfast table the next morning, Bill put his arm around my shoulders and apologized, contritely, saying, "Oh, Nell, we treat you so badly."

Typical of his New England roots, Bill was deeply patriotic and very proud of his wartime service in World War I. He liked to talk about those days, and did so often. I remember one morning, shortly after coming to the office, I was walking through Grand Central Station and ran into Bill, also on his way to the office. He asked if I'd like a cup of coffee. Sitting in the station coffee shop, he started reminiscing about World War I. I don't remember what triggered the topic of conversation—perhaps I had first shared some of my own recent service experience.

Anyway, he talked on and on, nostalgically and emotion-ally about that time in his life. Years later, I remember reading a letter Bill had written about 1941 or 1942 to Clarence S., an early member, announcing he was going to "join up." Clarence's answer to Bill was not to bother joining up himself, since *he* was doing it and he would carry the message. Bill answered gracefully that that would be fine. Bill shared his desire to reenter the Army as an officer—his status in World War I—with a fellow member in a good position to help in Washington, DC. The member did all he could, but it just didn't work out.

Bill was well-read. He was intellectual and philosophi-cal. In the Steps, Traditions, and Concepts, Bill consid-ered ideas, conceptual threads, and choices of action from diverse sources before zeroing in on the workable solution.

Bill was easy-going, generally agreeable, and accepting. He often spoke with a drawl. I have a vivid picture of him at home, even with company present, sprawled out over the floor register. Akron A.A.s attested to his favorite lounging area at Dr. Bob and Anne's being the living room floor. Dennis Manders, General Services' long-term Comptroller, remembers Bill at a drawn-out session of a General Service Conference, stretched out on the carpeted floor at the rear of the meeting room, napping.

But when it came to what he thought was necessary and good for the future of the Fellowship—such as the general service conference idea or the ratio change on the board of trustees—he was dogged, determined, and obstinate. He was relentlessly goal-minded, tunnel-visioned, and persistent.

As I mentioned, he didn't receive much encouragement on the idea of a general service conference from either the trustees or the membership. They universally opposed it for a long time. But this only made him more determined. So he went out and literally stumped the U.S. and Canada in the late forties, explaining and cajoling his listeners about the need for the continuity of the Fellowship after he and Dr. Bob were gone.

There were a couple of members, plus Henrietta Seiberling, who were unsympathetic to Bill. Believing he had "finally succumbed to madness," they contacted the membership themselves in 1950 to drum up opposition to the conference idea. They called themselves "the Orthodox Group." But they were rebuffed in their attempt to portray Bill as a madman. And, as I mentioned, the trustees did approve the conference, on a trial basis, at their October 1950 meeting.

Bill displayed the same obstinacy and persistence in his effort, lasting nearly eleven years, to get the ratio of the General Service Board changed to provide for a majority of alcoholic trustees. The old Alcoholic Foundation set up in 1938 had originally consisted of five members, three of them John D. Rockefeller, Jr.'s nonalcoholic friends, to ensure responsibility and continuity of the board in the days when sobriety for alcoholics was by no means certain. Besides the board of five, an advisory committee was created as part of the beginning structure. Both Bill and his brother-in-law, Dr. Strong, were among the eight members of that committee initially.

The board's structure was changed and enlarged so that by 1955 it numbered fifteen, eight of whom were nonalcoholics (Class A) and seven of whom were alcoholics (Class B). In the early fifties, Bill began to feel the time had come to change this ratio and he set about trying to get it changed. I remember a 1958 letter from Bill to nonalcoholic trustee Harrison Trice giving his reasons:

- The increased press of work with which we

have no business to saddle the nonalcoholic
members;
- Proper determination of A.A. policy and its
administration, which the nonalcoholics have
disclaimed ability to handle;
- Need for wider representation geographically
of alcoholic trustees;
- It is unsound psychologically for a movement
of our present size and maturity to take a
childish and fearful view that a majority of
alcoholics cannot be trusted to sit on our
most important board.

These points and his proposal were debated endlessly
by the trustees and wrangled over by the delegates at
conferences as Bill doggedly pursued his goal. Paradoxi-
cally, the membership was more opposed to the ratio
change than the trustees. Year after year, Bill's proposal
was tabled or the decision was passed along to the next
conference, until it finally came to a crucial vote in 1962.

The debate that year on his proposed ratio change was
long and ornery. The conference again postponed action
on it. Immediately following the vote they took a break.
Bill was sitting alone, and none of the delegates made a
move to go near him. As I looked at him across the room, I
never saw him so dejected and alone.

The rejection didn't discourage him for long, though.
At the following conferences, he went right back to
buttonholing delegates, explaining and persuading. In
fact, Dr. John Norris, chairman of the board, said that the
delegates were reacting not so much to the idea of the ratio
change as to Bill's tactics in pressuring them.

Finally, in 1966, the conference recommended "that the
Board be increased to 21, seven nonalcoholic and 14 alcoholic," as proposed the year before. The trustees unani-

mously accepted the recommendation.

Bill was overjoyed at the victory, but characteristically, he shared the credit quite rightly with Dr. Jack and especially with Herb M. in letters to each of them. His letter to Herb read in part:

> Without your good offices, your skill and your goodwill, nothing might have been accomplished . . . I know that A.A. of the future is going to be very greatly indebted to you for this contribution . . . during a difficult time in our pilgrim's progress.

I've mentioned Bill's depressions a couple of times before, but I'd like to say a few more words. It was a big part of his life from his school days on, but it was particularly troublesome during the decade, 1945–55. It always puzzled him why he had to endure this suffering since, as he often said, he was so fortunate and had so much to live and be grateful for. He felt sure it must be biochemical. Interestingly, this theory is supported more and more by medical, psychiatric, and scientific opinion. He described his depressive episodes as manic-depressive. It did seem to be true that his most crippling depressions followed periods of intense emotional and physical activity, when he was expending enormous amounts of psychic and spiritual energy.

All of us close to Bill—particularly Lois, Dr. Jack, Herb M., and myself—were concerned. But outsiders were often less sympathetic. I witnessed the criticism he received from some A.A. members who would suggest caustically that if he got to meetings and followed his own Twelve Steps, he would be out of trouble. Bill agreed. He not only tried valiantly to do just that (he took his Fifth Step with his spiritual sponsor, Fr. Ed Dowling), but he also sought help from every other avenue he could think of.

In the middle 1950s, Bill's friend Gerald Heard introduced him to two English psychiatrists, Drs. Humphrey
Osmond and Abram Hoffer. They were working with
schizophrenics and alcoholic patients at a Canadian hospital, experimenting with a synthetic chemical called lysergic
acid diethylamide—LSD. Later, in the sixties, LSD would
become notorious as a street drug, but in the fifties, there
were no laws or regulations governing its usage. The
psychiatrists reported that it was producing some beneficial
effects in their patients, particularly in shortening their
resistance to treatment. Bill became enthusiastic about the
potential, saying, "Anything that helps alcoholics is good
and shouldn't be dismissed out of hand."

While visiting California in the late fifties, Bill took
some of the chemical, under the supervision of his friend,
Gerald Heard. Returning home, he continued to experi-
ment with it. I tried some myself, as did Lois (a very small
amount), and others. Bill followed closely the scientific
results of administering LSD to mental patients and alcoholics over the next two or three years. He withdrew from
the experiments completely by 1959, when it was apparent that the whole idea conflicted with his position as a
founder and father image in A.A.

Bill continued his friendship with Drs. Hoffer and
Osmond, closely following their work. In the early 1960s,
they reported some success in treating depressives with
massive doses of vitamin B-3, also called niacin. Bill tried
the vitamin himself and found, to his joy, that it helped
him greatly. In fact, he told me it was the first time he was
experiencing life as a normal person must feel it. As Bill
became excited about niacin, he shared his enthusiasm
with doctor friends in A.A. and much more widely with
A.A. members. He put together three papers about B-3 to
help spread the word.

All this caused a big flap among many in the Fellowship. Members and trustees alike spoke out against what they viewed as Bill's "using A.A." to promote this new, personal cause of his. It was true that niacin advocates began voicing their enthusiasm at A.A. meetings, while those opposed to it used the meetings as a forum to express their views. So it was evident that Bill, without intending to, was violating two of the Traditions: the Sixth, that A.A. ought never endorse or lend its name to any outside enterprise, and the Tenth, that A.A. has no opinion on outside issues, hence the A.A. name ought never be drawn into public controversy. So the decision was made at the 1967 conference as proposed by the board of trustees that all inquiries and activities relating to vitamin B-3 should be handled outside of the G.S.O. by a separate office using separate stationery.

I knew from taking niacin myself (briefly—depression wasn't a problem with me and I didn't like the flushing it caused) and from our correspondence with a large number of A.A. members that it could have beneficial effects. Bill continued to take niacin the rest of his life (so did Lois) and to share his enthusiasm with others. I have heard many A.A. visitors come up to Bill and thank him for saving their lives twice. After Bill passed away and during the years since, both Lois and I continued to receive calls and letters asking about Bill's success in relieving depression by taking niacin. I always share what I can of Bill's experience, and several members have thanked me profusely for passing along this helpful information.

Bill was extraordinarily open-minded and inquisitive. He was a seeker. He had a long-time fascination with psychic phenomena. This was also in keeping with his absolute faith in the afterlife. Incidentally, Dr. Bob and Anne S. were also interested in psychic phenomena—and so am I.

In the early forties, Bill and Lois often held meetings—
or "spook sessions," as they termed them—in a small
downstairs bedroom at Stepping Stones. A.A. friends, a
couple of Rockefeller people, and even some Bedford Hills
neighbors frequently participated in these sessions and
experienced unusual phenomena. For example, during
one evening sitting, Bill spelled out slowly, letter by letter,
a paragraph or two from a sermon by St. Boniface which
was verified by Rev. Willard Richardson.

One of Bill's most convincing experiences took place in
1947 during their first visit to Nantucket Island. They
arrived at night and Bill rose early the next morning.
While sitting alone in his host's kitchen with a cup of
coffee, he had lengthy conversations with three Nantuck-
eters who had lived more than a hundred years before: a
whaler, a sailor who said his name was David Morrow
and that he had been killed serving under Admiral Farra-
gut at the Battle of Mobile Bay, and a sea captain named
Pettingill. "Just for fun, I told this story at breakfast," Bill
shared later with a friend, "making pointed reference to
the names." Their host was skeptical to say the least, and
the matter was dropped.

The next day, Bill, Lois, and their hosts were meeting
others for a picnic, having set a rendezvous at the head of
Nantucket's main street. At that spot was a small monument to Nantucket's fallen in the Civil War, and at the foot
of the monument the names of the dead were chiseled.
One of them was David Morrow. Bill called his host's
attention to it. The next day, they visited the Nantucket
Whaling Museum for the first time. There, in an open
book, were the names of the masters of the old whaling
vessels. One of them was Pettingill. "There isn't even a
remote chance that I had at some time read or heard about
all three of these ordinary former inhabitants of the

island," Bill wrote. "Maybe one but certainly not three."[12]

In the 1950s, Duke University became the center of experiments in precognition and researchers assembled extensive records of extrasensory perception. Bill corresponded with Dr. J.B. Rhine of Duke regarding these subjects, and shared some of his own experiences. I have continued to be avidly interested in these subjects myself.

Bill was loyal all his life to his native Vermont. He returned several times a year, and Lois often drove up with him in their jeep. They stayed at the Londonderry Inn or the Equinox Hotel in Manchester. They walked a lot, talked, worked on their separate writing projects for A.A. and Al-Anon, and also counseled people. These included A.A.s, Al-Anons, and others whom they had simply come to know. Bill returned home from these trips refreshed, ready to do battle again with the trustees. He would bring back drafts of memos and *Grapevine* articles ready for me to type. And he would usually bring back more of those Vermont stories to share with us.

My first visit to Vermont was with Bill and Lois in the fall of 1960. The occasion was the twenty-fifth anniversary of A.A. in Vermont, and the place was Burlington. Bill and Lois were the guests of honor, and Dr. Bob and Anne were honored *in absentia*, as Vermont was also Dr. Bob's home state. Bill received a citation on behalf of A.A. from then-Governor Stafford. Bill and Lois were in top form and enjoyed it thoroughly. Tapes of that weekend are in the A.A. Archives. This was a rewarding occasion for me also. I accompanied Lois to Al-Anon meetings and spent time listening to the affecting stories shared by spouses.

The occasion of my second visit to Vermont was Bill's burial and memorial service in East Dorset on May 8, 1971. Lois' brother Rogers, who had introduced her to

Bill, had died in December 1970, about a month before Bill, so he was interred a few days before Bill but in another nearby cemetery. Lois visited Rogers' grave on this visit also. I remember Dr. Jack was at Bill's service, and gave a very moving eulogy at graveside.

During another trip with a friend, I made a point of walking around the old Manchester Airport, site of one of Bill's more famous drunken adventures. The year was 1929, before Bill's sobriety. Bill and Ebby had been partying all night in Albany, and they hired another drinking friend, Ted Burke, to fly them to Manchester the next day in his plane. The airport at Manchester was just being completed, but had not yet been used. Bill or the pilot called ahead to Manchester to tell them they were coming. The excited Manchester folks got together the town band and a committee to welcome the historic first flight to land at their brand-new airport. The delegation was headed by Mrs. Orvis, the owner of the famous Equinox House.

Bill later wrote that on the way to Manchester in the plane the three of them had been "pulling at a bottle. We circled the field and somehow lit on the meadow. The welcoming delegation charged forward. It was up to Ebby and me to do something . . . We managed to slide out of the cockpit, [and] fell on the ground, where we lay, immobile. Such was the history-making episode of the first airplane ever to land at Manchester, Vermont."[13]

6

BILL'S "SHORTCOMINGS AND CHARACTER DEFECTS"

Over the last fifteen years or so, I've been invited to A.A. gatherings to share my memories of Bill and Lois and the Fellowship's early history. After listening to me at one such gathering, a member asked, "Didn't Bill have any character defects at all?" I was momentarily taken aback. I must say I'm uneasy discussing in public anyone else's "defects," including Bill's. I had perhaps gone overboard on his good points, creating the impression of divine infallibility. So I hastened to reply, "Well, yes, of course he did." After all, he was human. In fact, an A.A. friend used to say, "he wore his halo a bit on the jaunty side."

Bill often talked about his shortcomings. Here's part of a letter he wrote to Vern V. in 1952.

> My grandfather used to have a saying, "it takes all kinds of folks to make a world." Nothing is more true for Alcoholics Anonymous. Each group and each individual has special defects of

character. . . . That goes for all of us, of course. Each time I severely criticize anyone, I usually discover that, in some form or other, I have the same fault myself. Or maybe I'm criticizing in order to feel a little superior to those I'm attacking. It is usually one motive or the other. Happily, though, these frictions of ours are but the pains which cause us all to grow up. They don't do a bit of harm in the long run. . . .

I believe his most obvious character defect—one he spoke about himself—was his power driving. Once he got his teeth into an idea or proposal that he considered necessary and good for A.A.'s future, he seldom let go until he had pushed it through. He could be really tenacious and stubborn. And he had absolute tunnel vision on these subjects. That is the way he was able to accomplish what he did. Bill was always battling apathy, ultraconservatism, the trustees, or factions within the Fellowship who did not agree with him.

"Bill was not much for small talk," said our co-worker, Dennis Manders. "You could carry on a spirited conversation with him as long as you stuck to the subject he was hot on at the moment. If you tried to shift to another subject, he might simply walk away." He could be a poor listener if the topic of conversation didn't interest him. When he was on one of his crusades, his eyes and mind were fixed on the goal and he was impatient to come to decisions as soon as possible.

He was also a dedicated, tireless talker. Many weekends at Stepping Stones, with company present, I remember Bill leaning back in a straight chair, arms in motion, holding the floor as he expounded on whatever aspect of A.A. was currently engaging his attention—the Conference, the trustee ratio, or the Concepts. Not many people interrupted him once he got started. When Lois tried, he would shoot a slight frown in her direction. When he tried the same tactic with me, I pretended I didn't notice and, typically, barged right in with my own comments.

A family member recalled, a bit irritably, that holiday visits were too often given over to Bill's long monologues on A.A. But this was Bill's way of refining and defining new issues—verbalizing them and noting reactions before he set them to paper. Of course, this didn't help those who had to sit and listen for long periods of time, particularly around holidays.

When he was trying to convince you in an argument, he was not above a little arm twisting, as many people can attest. If he felt the issue needed an immediate decision and you still disagreed, he could really pound at you, backing you into a verbal corner. As he went on and on, you wanted to retaliate in anger. He was sometimes his own worst enemy because this kind of behavior just made it more difficult to get his message across or accepted.

Many members recall Bill's tendency to exaggerate. Ruth Hock, Bill's secretary and office manager, remembers that when talking before a meeting he was prone to be overgenerous in quoting the latest membership count or convention attendance. He might say, for example, "Well, folks, I'm glad to say there are now 150 members." Ruth, who like me could be quite literal-minded, would lean over and whisper, "No, Bill, it's only 95" or whatever the figure was. Afterward, Bill would complain good-naturedly, "Oh, Ruth, you're spoiling my fun." Bill always claimed that the attendance at the 1955 International Convention in St. Louis was 5,000. Dennis, who handled the registrations, told me the true figure was about 3,100, plus possibly a few hundred walk-ins. I recall myself that the crowd nowhere near filled Kiel Auditorium.

Bill was not always tactful. He was often blunt. And he sometimes lacked a sense of confidentiality. If you had a secret, it wouldn't do to share it immediately with him because he was likely to blurt it out unless you made him raise his right hand and hope to die.

He could be absentminded, and this was, I believe, part of his tunnel vision. In 1950, the office moved from 415 Lexington Avenue around the corner to 141 East Forty-fourth Street. Bill would arrive from Bedford Hills into Grand Central Station on the commuter train. Thinking of weightier matters, he would bound through the station and across Lexington with those long strides of his, and head directly into the old building. The elevator operator would hurry over to him saying, "No, no, Mr. W. You're located around the corner now." This happened not once, but many times.

Bill was somewhat wary of new technology and new techniques. When it was decided to make a home-movie style documentary, *Bill's Own Story*, he had a kind of stage fright in front of the camera. As comfortable as he was with words and talking, he felt awkward and uncomfortable in the presence of that unblinking eye and the mikes suspended overhead. I was there at Stepping Stones the day the filming started and I remember how Bill fussed, finding all kinds of reasons why a particular scene wouldn't work. However, when they got down to filming, Bill and Lois' lack of professionalism added to the charm of the film.

What Bill felt about cameras, he also felt about new dictating machines. Until the very end, we were using a pair of antique dictating machines, then about 22 years old. Not only were they no longer being manufactured, the plastic discs were no longer made either. But Bill felt comfortable with his antique machine.

His persistence and power driving were interpreted by many as coming from a large ego. What amazed me during the years around Bill, and even more in retrospect, is that someone with such a healthy ego could sublimate it in all his actions: discounting his own contributions, insisting on the cofounder concept, always sharing credit with others, turning down public honors, and eschewing power and glory.

Sam Shoemaker, in a letter to Bill, summed it up pretty well, I thought, when he said:

> God has saved you from the love of the spot-light, Bill—at least, if not from the love of it, from getting too much into it. It is one of the biggest things about you, and I often speak of it.

To some members, Bill's failure to attend A.A. meetings regularly was a grievous fault. He regarded it as such himself. But the Fellowship just wouldn't allow this cofounder to attend meetings as an ordinary A.A. member. That was one of the disappointments of Bill's A.A. life, for he desperately wanted the healing, the insights, and the spiritual renewal that ordinary members find at meetings. When Bill did drop in at a meeting, he was always asked to speak. He was either lionized or subjected to unsolicited advice about what should be done about certain issues—or both. That meant that Bill was always giving, never taking.

Of course at Stepping Stones he was surrounded by A.A.s and Al-Anons, both in person and by phone. And I recall an endless procession of people seeking his personal Twelfth Stepping or his advice in their later sobriety—and the endless hours he devoted to them. For Bill, Twelfth Step work was part of being Bill. And in many ways being Bill was a lonely occupation.

7

BILL'S OUTSIDE FRIENDS

Most A.A. members regarded Bill with a kind of super-reverence that was entirely unrealistic. He suffered anxiety about his ability to live up to their expectations. And, when he failed to live up to members' expectations, many didn't hesitate to express their disappointment, both in letters and in person. It was unrealistic to expect him to absorb this criticism without feeling hurt, although it seldom showed. He was philosophical about criticism. He listened and learned from it. He maintained a healthy perspective in regard to the adulation and denigration he often received.

It is not surprising that, in difficult situations, Bill often reached out to nonalcoholics with whom he was in close contact. He could share his deep concerns and draw upon their strength and understanding as he could rarely do with fellow A.A. members, especially if a problem concerned the leadership.

Perhaps the most important of Bill's early friends, and the one with whom he was most frequently in touch, was Fr. Edward Dowling, S.J. It is impossible to overestimate the role Fr. Ed played as Bill's "spiritual sponsor." He appeared in Bill's life, as if sent by a Higher Power, on a dismal, rainy night in 1940 when Bill and Lois were at their lowest ebb financially and A.A. was going through much turmoil and growing pains. Not only did they talk far into the night at their first meeting in that little room at the old Twenty-fourth Street Clubhouse, but Bill continued ever afterward to lean on this special friend for spiritual strength, comfort, and advice. Ed was a man of great warmth and good humor, whose compassionate ministry to alcoholics in St. Louis gave him a unique understanding of Bill's pain and problems.

I admired Fr. Ed myself because he was direct and full of humor. He exuded spirituality and humility. He was of medium height with a wide "map of Ireland" face, twinkling eyes, a shock of white hair, and a friendly manner. Because of a limp, he walked with a cane. This cane and the personal crucifix he wore were given to Bill after Fr. Ed died in his sleep on April 2, 1960. They were among Bill's favorite and most cherished possessions, and are still to be seen in his studio at Stepping Stones. He and Bill met often and corresponded regularly. Bill confided in and shared his feelings with Fr. Ed more than any other friend.

Dr. Harry Tiebout and Bill enjoyed a long and close relationship that benefited Bill on several levels. Bill went to Dr. Tiebout for therapy for his depression in the middle forties. He reported that the experience had helped him understand his problem and live within his limitations, but it didn't do much to relieve the depressive state.

Dr. Tiebout was one of the first psychiatrists to recognize the effectiveness of A.A. in his work with alcoholics, and his professional support was tremendously helpful in persuading other psychiatrists of A.A.'s worth. In 1939, Dr. Tiebout had seen spectacular A.A. recoveries in two of his patients, Marty M. and her friend Grennie C. Along with Drs. Kirby Collier and Foster Kennedy, he was responsible for arranging for Bill to speak before two medical societies, which gave the program a big boost at the time. He also authored professional papers that analyzed, from a psychiatric viewpoint, why A.A. worked so well, and he served as a Class A trustee of A.A.'s General Service Board from 1957 until his death in 1966.

Bill had great admiration and respect for Harry and used him as a sounding board for his ideas. With a psychiatrist's objectivity and insight, Harry recognized that the Fellowship as a whole was less emotionally mature than Bill believed. He helped prevent Bill from turning over his responsibility and authority to the groups before they were ready to accept it. As far back as 1950, Bill was proclaiming enthusiastically that "A.A. has come of age." And Harry cautioned, "Not yet." Harry was a rather heavyset, genial man, easy to know, full of humor, and firm in his convictions.

Another doctor who was a good friend of Bill's was E.M. Jellinek, Ph.D.—"Bunky" to Bill and others who knew him well. Dr. Jellinek was world famous as *the* scientific / medical authority on alcoholism. He cofounded the National Committee for Education on Alcoholism and founded the Yale Center of Alcohol Studies, which later moved to Rutgers University in New Jersey. The author of *The Disease Concept of Alcoholism*, he did the basic modern research in this field. He developed the famous Jellinek Chart, the curve showing the progression of the illness and subsequent recovery. He and Bill had great admiration for each other. At Jellinek's invitation, Bill spoke at the Yale Center in the early forties. And when they encountered each other at alcoholism seminars or professional meetings, they enjoyed joking together. After Jellinek died in 1972, Rutgers posthumously awarded Bill the first Jellinek Award. It sits on top of the filing cabinet in Bill's studio at Stepping Stones.

Mr. Hanford Twitchell, a nonalcoholic and well-known professional man in New York, knew Bill well in those Oxford Group days of 1935–36. He often accompanied Bill to Towns Hospital and to Calvary Mission where Bill talked to alcoholics. Reminiscing about Bill, he remembered that at first Bill was alone, and didn't seem especially a part of the Oxford Group meetings, but that soon changed because people would follow him. He was always more interested in talking to drunks during and after the Oxford Group meetings than in carrying their message as a team member. He says Bill believed that for the alcoholic to be helped he needed to gain some degree of spiritual belief, if he didn't already have it, and that the one-to-one relationship so strongly advocated by Oxford Group founder Frank Buchman was especially important in helping someone to stay sober. Bill wanted only to be concerned with the recovery of alcoholics in the Oxford Group, while Buchman wanted to save the world. This is where they differed.

Years later, Sam Shoemaker acknowledged Bill's preference for the company of alcoholics and in a very moving and humble letter, said:

> Bill, if you ever write the story of A.A.'s early connection with Calvary, I think it ought to be said that in all honesty, we were coached in the feeling that you were off on your own spur, trying to do something by yourself, and out of the mainstream of the work. I remember that very well; you got your inspiration from those early days, but you didn't get much encouragement from any of us . . . fortunately it didn't keep you from going on and beginning what

was this amazing contribution to one of the vast needs of this day. . . .

There were several other Oxford Group people who, in those early days of the late thirties, recognized Bill's potential contributions and expressed their admiration to him and to other friends. I remember well the supportive letters and visits he received from John Ryder, who was very active in the Oxford Group in the thirties. The Rev. Willard Hunter is still a friend to many A.A.s and they are still in communication with him. Over the years, Willard and his Oxford Group friend Jim Newton have shared their insights and memories of the Oxford Group experience with many others.

In May 1935, when Bill's business proxy fight in Akron had failed and he felt an urgent need to talk to a fellow alcoholic, it was Henrietta Seiberling who put him in touch with Dr. Bob. The two soon-to-be cofounders met in the gatehouse of the Seiberling estate. Henrietta was not an alcoholic. She was a friend of Anne's and a member of the Oxford Group, where she had tried in vain to help Dr. Bob overcome his drinking problem by applying Oxford Group philosophy and concepts. And as the first small group of recovering alcoholics met with the Oxford Group in Akron, Henrietta was directly involved with them.

From the beginning, she was critical of Bill for what she considered his large ego, for one thing. And, apparently, his lack of sophistication and some "country-style" mannerisms, annoyed her. I think she had little knowledge or even understanding, later on, of the intensity and extent of his efforts and accomplishments on behalf of A.A. Perhaps there was some jealousy on her part, but Bill always recognized her contributions. I honestly don't know to this day what her overall objections to Bill's leadership were. She just seemed to be against what he was doing at any given time.

Bill, on the other hand, was tolerant of—and almost oblivious to—Henrietta's hostility. He was unfailingly gracious to her, always making sure she was invited to his annual A.A. anniversary dinners in New York and other A.A. events. When she accepted, he introduced her from the podium, expressing his deep gratitude for the important role she had played in A.A.'s beginnings.

In time, Henrietta and I communicated, via telephone mainly, on a friendly basis. I remember visiting her at her home once, after she moved east, and she visited our writing and research office when it was located at 305 East Forty-fifth Street. Later, she stopped in to visit and inspect our then small archives office at 468 Park Avenue South, on the eighth floor.

I treasure Lois' and my friendship with Irving and Julie Harris. Irv wrote a book of his own about the Oxford Group days called *The Breeze of the Spirit*, in which he also describes Bill and the beginnings of A.A. Irv was a close friend of Sam Shoemaker, and was especially helpful to Sam in the continuation of the spirit of the Oxford Group movement, which after his break with Buchman in 1941 they called "Faith at Work." Irv did a newsletter called "Faith at Work" for several years, and always sent Bill and Lois copies and kept them up to date on what was happening.

Interestingly, on re-reading parts of Irving's book recently, I noted on page 137, he describes the origin of the name "Faith at Work," as taken from Sam's emphasis on Christianity as a "religion that works." I remember that early A.A. members described A.A. as a success because "It works," and supposedly our name for the first publishing company in 1939, "Works Publishing," derived from the same source. Also, a favorite quotation of Anne S.'s, from the Bible, "Faith without works is dead," could have been a source, too. Irving passed on in July 1990; a sad loss. But I'm grateful Julie remains nearby.

Back in the early thirties, shortly before Bill's alcoholism took over completely, financier Joe Hirshhorn employed Bill to analyze and evaluate companies in which Hirshhorn might invest. Although Hirshhorn tolerated Bill long after others were down on him because of his drunken behavior, they too parted company after Bill disgraced himself on an assignment for Joe in Canada.

The two men lost touch for more than 25 years. Joe became a man of enormous wealth and a noted art collector. His estate in Greenwich, CT, was a virtual museum of modern art, surrounded by lovely statues and other sculptures bordering the lawns. Bill and Lois visited there frequently in the sixties, their homes being within easy driving distance of each other.

In 1962, Bill had just about ended his direct participation in A.A. affairs, other than on an informal basis. He began to devote more time to interests outside of A.A. and resumed in a limited way his Wall Street activity. At about this time, he ran into Joe at Kennedy Airport. Soon, the two men began talking together regularly on investments and stock ventures. Their renewed association was, I know, gratifying to them both.

I remember Bill talking about Joe's desire to leave his art collection to a museum. After a lot of consideration, Joe finally chose Washington, DC, where a modern building was erected to house all the wonderful art and sculpture. This new museum is located near the old Smithsonian building on the Mall. After Bill's death Joe and his wife remained in contact with Lois. He invited Lois to the opening ceremonies of the new museum in the early eighties.

I think also of Dr. John L. Norris, who left us in January 1989, and of his long, devoted service to A.A., both in the alcoholism field and to the A.A. General Service Board. The same is true of Austin MacCormick and Bernard Smith. Their contributions to A.A. from the early forties on are enormous and lasting, as are those of the very special early supporters of Bill: Mr. Rockefeller, Jr., and his friends.

Col. Ed Towns, who later took over management of Towns Hospital from his father, Charles Towns, wrote to Bill after his own retirement in 1960:

My part in your program I feel was a tribute to "Pop" Towns, who believed in A.A. from the start and considered you a man of destiny.

I remember the uplift and excitement we experienced from letters, from personal visits to the office, and from listening to Bill share memories of his first contacts with two professional men overseas: Henk Krauweel and Dr. Gordon Johnson. An important social worker in Holland, Henk Krauweel met Bill and Lois during their visit to Holland in 1950, and the two men became good friends. Henk had a lot to do with translating the Twelve Steps into Dutch. He gave the small beginnings of A.A. in that country a big boost and became a leading authority on alcoholism in Europe. I remember his visit to the office and meeting him in the early fifties. Dr. Johnson, a leading psychiatrist in Oslo, Norway, and according to Bill, a deeply religious man, contributed so much to the start of A.A. in his country. Upon returning from a visit to Norway, Bill reported that Dr. Johnson saw the implications of the Twelve Steps and "he threw the whole weight of his reputation behind the uncertain little group." Bill continued his contact with these two good friends for many years. A friend and colleague of Dr. Johnson, Dr.

Oscar Olsen, has likewise been a close and enthusiastic friend of A.A. since 1947 and attended the Seattle Convention in 1990.

Considering the characterization of alcoholics in the thirties and forties as amoral, despicable sots, it's amazing to me how many professional people outside of A.A.—doctors, lawyers, educators, religious leaders, and sociologists—early on recognized the value of the Fellowship's program. For these professionals to comprehend the nature of alcoholism as an illness, to understand what A.A. was striving to accomplish as early as 1937, I think is truly remarkable.

Other long-time, special friends of Bill were Jack Alexander (he wrote the two famous articles on A.A. in the *Saturday Evening Post* in 1941 and 1950 and was a member of the Board of Trustees in the early fifties) and Rev. Harry Emerson Fosdick, the well-known minister of the Riverside Church in New York. He favorably reviewed the Big Book when it was first published, but confessed at A.A.'s Eighth Anniversary Dinner on November 24, 1943, that "he wouldn't know a gin rickey from a small beer!" Fulton Oursler, editor of *Liberty* magazine in 1939 and member of the Board of Trustees later on, was another good friend. So was Albert Scott, chairman of the board of the Riverside Church. To raise money for the publication of the Big Book, he distributed a couple of chapters from the unpublished work to friends. He also voiced the opinion, mentioned earlier, that too much money would spoil the Fellowship. He believed it should be self-supporting as soon as possible. Dr. Russell Blaisdell, head of the Rockland State Hospital, invited Bill to speak there in December 1939 (we have Bill's talk in our archives; it's a great talk). He was also present at the Rockefeller dinner on February 8, 1940, given on behalf of A.A.

Another early friend, Eugene Exman, religious editor at Harper and Brothers, encouraged publication of the Big Book after reading the first two chapters and offering a $1,500 advance. This offer was turned down, as Bill and the emerging group decided instead to publish the book themselves.

Among those outside friends who gave, as Bill put it, a "long season of service," was Leonard V. Harrison, director of public affairs of the Community Service Society of New York City for many years. Leonard came on as a trustee of the board in 1941, and except for a five-year hiatus, served until April 1961. From 1956 to 1961, he was chairman. "He saw A.A. through its frightfully wobbly time of adolescence," Bill said of him in *Alcoholics Anonymous Comes of Age*, "a time when nobody could say whether our society would hang together or blow up entirely. What his wise counsel and steady hand meant to us of A.A. in that stormy period is quite beyond telling."[14]

Warden Clinton T. Duffy of San Quentin Prison was another of those nonalcoholics whose friendship Bill valued. In late 1943, Bill and Lois made an ambitious cross-country trip to California, where they visited Bill's mother, Dr. Emily Strobell, in San Diego. Bill spoke to more than 1,000 A.A.s in Los Angeles. In San Francisco, he met Duffy, the first corrections official in the country to permit, as far as we know, the founding of an A.A. meeting inside prison walls.

After spending the Christmas holidays with Bill's mother, Bill and Lois drove to Trabuco College in the California desert. Trabuco had been founded by Gerald Heard, the British philosopher, anthropologist, metaphysician, radio commentator, and mystery novelist whom Dave D., a California A.A. member, had been anxious for Bill to meet. Bill and Gerald struck up an immediate friendship.

I believe it was through Gerald Heard that Bill met Aldous Huxley, author of *Brave New World*, teacher, and philosopher. Again, Bill and Huxley had an immediate rapport. Aldous called Bill "the greatest social architect of the century." They carried on a lively correspondence for nearly two decades.

I remember seeing Huxley on one of his trips to New York in the forties when he visited the General Service Office to see Bill. He was a tall, impressive-looking man, and rather hunched-over. Both Huxley and Heard wrote articles for the *Grapevine*. Huxley's article, "Man and Reality," appeared in the souvenir book *A.A. Today*, distributed at the 1960 International Convention in Long Beach. Heard's article "The Search for Ecstasy," which defined A.A. as an ad hoc church, appeared in the May 1958 issue of the *Grapevine*. When Huxley died in 1963, his widow wrote a long letter about his death to the family and included a copy for Bill, possibly the only person outside his family to receive it.

Bill, Dave D., Heard, Huxley, and philanthropists David and Lucille Kahn all had an interest in mysticism and psychic phenomena. Heard and Huxley were close to the Kahns, who themselves were long-time friends and supporters of Edgar Cayce, the famous psychic. Bill, occasionally with Lois, enjoyed meeting with them at the Kahns' apartment on Central Park South in New York City.

I visited Lucille recently. Still a beautiful, gracious lady, she continues to reside at her apartment, her husband having passed away several years ago. We reminisced about Bill's visits. She remembered the shyness, the gentleness, and the essential loneliness deep inside Bill and the gratitude he expressed for all their friendship and sharing, understanding, and counseling.

75

She described an evening when all were in town, sitting around the fire in the large living room fireplace, when the conversation turned to helping Bill cope with his isolation in A.A. They talked about meditation as well as receiving the spiritual input that came from close friends. Actually, Bill did meditate frequently with Lois during their morning quiet time and with other friends. He and Lois often joined our meditation group on Friday evenings in nearby Chappaqua, at the home of Anne and Devoe B.

From time to time Bill talked about the "cofounder business" with other friends in similar situations who could understand what he was experiencing. In 1959 he wrote to Robert H. about loneliness:

> For quite different reasons, I share your feelings of being rather alone at times—alone amid thousands of well-wishers. The fact is I have never been able to join A.A. myself. I can't participate in the meetings as others do. People either wish to depend upon me or maybe to dominate me. So the co-founder business is sort of abnormal but I suppose a necessary state of affairs. Anyhow, I feel as you do; I've got more to be thankful for than anybody else in the world. . . .

All of this was happening at the time Bill was in the process of turning over all decision-making to the Fellowship itself. The timing was right, for within a few years Bill's emphysema would catch up with him.

As Dennis Manders correctly prophesied at the St. Louis Convention, Bill's final stepping down from leadership would take a few more years. And in 1962 he did just that.

8

BILL AND DR. BOB

Dr. Bob
Simplicity, devotion, steadfastness, and loyalty;
these were the hallmarks of Dr. Bob's character
which he has well implanted in so many of us.[15]
Bill

Bill W.
It was five years ago I first met you, Bill . . . I
shall never forget, nor cease to be grateful.[16]
Dr. Bob

I never tired of hearing Bill tell the story of how Henrietta
Seiberling told him about Dr. Bob on that fateful Saturday
in Akron, and how they finally met the next afternoon at
the Seiberling gatehouse. When I became the A.A. archivist, I hoped that sooner or later I might come across some
written documentation of the meeting.

Finally, in the late seventies, I found what I was looking
for, or rather, Lois did. It happened on a weekend visit to
Stepping Stones. Lois excitedly asked me to read a newly
discovered collection of letters, stowed away for years
down in the cellar, that Bill had written to her from Akron
during that summer of 1935. For Lois, the re-reading

brought back the happiness and disappointment of that time: happiness that Bill was sober and making friends; disappointment that he did not return as soon as she expected.

As I read through them, excitement took hold when I found in my hand the very letter that Bill had written to Lois on that fateful Mother's Day in May 1935. He wrote, "Today I met a man who has my problem."

Regrettably, I saw Dr. Bob only once and then very briefly. It was in the fall of 1948, when he joined Bill and Lois at the annual Intergroup Dinner in New York, one of the rare joint appearances of the two men. Dr. Bob came to the office. Our small office was packed like a sardine can that day. I was on duty at the receptionist's desk and switchboard and was momentarily called away on an errand. Apparently I missed him, because the only picture I have in my mind is of this tall, husky, slightly stooped man going down the hall to the exit. So my only clear memory of him is from the rear! However, I feel I know both Dr. Bob and Anne very well indeed having heard Bill and Lois and other A.A. friends talk about them so often over the years.

Dr. Bob became, as Bill described him, "the prince of Twelfth Steppers"—a title for which he was well qualified. It grew out of his natural instinct as a doctor for helping people and his intense desire as an alcoholic to administer to his fellow sufferers. I thought of him as cautious by nature, not given to hasty opinions. Bob often urged caution on Bill as well. Although he shared Bill's vision of A.A.'s future, he felt no action should be taken until complete agreement had been secured in advance. Though he didn't always agree with the timing of Bill's projects and proposals, Bob always backed him up. Bill, on the other hand, felt that any innovative step or action for better functioning of the Fellowship in the future should be tried. If it didn't work, it could be dropped. But the effort should be made. I've heard Bill say many times that one wouldn't be faulted for not succeeding with any goal, only for not trying hard enough.

The temperaments and personalities of the two cofounders differed. By nature, Bob was more reserved in public than Bill, but in private he was more gregarious. Early members in Akron described him as always one of the boys. He liked to play cards and watch fights on TV. He liked cars and drove them fast. But he didn't particularly like to speak at large gatherings. Bill was just the opposite. He was a more public man.

From the beginning of their relationship, Bill and Bob felt close and protective of each other, even though they were widely separated by distance for long periods of time. Bob worried about Bill's health, and Bill worried about Bob's money situation. Dr. Bob was spending so much time treating alcoholics, for which he would take no compensation, that his regular practice had all but dried up. Bill, in partnership with Hank P., had formed Works Publishing Company in early 1939 to publish the Big Book. At Bill's insistence, a major condition of their turning over their interest in Works Publishing to the Alcoholic Foundation in 1940 was that Bob and Anne would receive a royalty on the Big Book for the rest of their lives.

Bob, however, was mindful of Bill and Lois' unstable financial condition and insisted that Bill take some part of his (Bob's) royalty when he needed it. For the first year or two, the Big Book wasn't selling well, so neither received royalties. After that discouraging period, however, the book started to sell, and when the book debts were repaid, both Bill and Bob received royalties from the foundation. Bob's were retroactive to 1940.

In 1939, Bill made an effort to obtain financial relief for Bob by asking for a grant from the Guggenheim Foundation in New York. He wrote in part:

At Akron, Ohio, there is a physician, Dr. Robert H. S————, who has been responsible during the last 4 years for the recovery of at least 100 chronic alcoholics of types hitherto regarded by the medical profession as hopeless . . . without charge to sufferers, without fanfare and almost without funds . . . Because of his great amount of voluntary alcoholic work the doctor has been unable to rebuild his surgical practice. If he continues alcoholic work at the present pace, he may lose the remainder of his practice, probably his home. Obviously, he should continue, but how?

Bill then suggested a stipend of $3,000 for one year, reassuring the foundation that other efforts were being made to provide necessary funds. He closed the letter with the words, "He knows nothing of this approach on his behalf."

The Guggenheim Foundation replied, holding out little hope of being able to accommodate Dr. Bob, since their fellowships were given to creative and original works in the arts. Bill was sufficiently discouraged that he let the matter drop.

Both Bill and Bob shared a rollicking sense of humor. They loved to tease. They liked to tell stories, and they were both good at it. Bob was noted for using little parables to make his points. They both enjoyed giving people nicknames, including each other. Bill almost always called Bob "Doc" or "Smithy." Dr. Bob called Bill "Willie" or "Sir William." Occasionally, in letters to Ruth Hock at the office, he was simply "that guy," as in "Tell that guy to write when you see him." (Bill wasn't the most consistent correspondent in the world.)

Both Bob and Bill had been involved in the Oxford Group before they met—Bill, in the months after he emerged from Towns Hospital and Dr. Bob, seeking help for his drinking problem from the Akron Oxford Group at the urging of his wife, Anne, and Henrietta Seiberling. When Bob and Bill started trying out their ideas for bringing sobriety to other alcoholics, they followed the Oxford Group format.

Bob would share his own story on his first contact with the prospect in the hospital, to establish identification. This custom was also followed by subsequent early members in Akron. Like Bill and Lois who shared their home with alcoholics in New York, Bob and Anne often took new prospects to live at their home in the early days. Members gathered there informally as well as attending the Oxford Group meetings at the home of T. Henry and Clarace Williams. Early members described how, at their meeting, Bob liked to sit with an open Bible on his lap, out of which a passage would be selected at random and read. A discussion would then follow on its relevance to the personal problems of those present. The emphasis was on day-to-day living, how to cope with personal problems, and self-examination. Alcoholism as an illness was also discussed. Guidance (an Oxford Group term) was nearly always asked for and listened to.

Apparently the "alcoholic squad" met separately from the regular Oxford Group, though they opened and closed the meeting jointly. Before joining the meeting of the "alcoholic squad," a newcomer was asked if he wanted to make a surrender, a first and crucial decision. If the answer was yes, or something approximating it, the new person was taken upstairs by Dr. Bob and/or a couple of other members. The surrender was made on his knees, and they all came back downstairs, the newcomer usually pale and shaken, as was his spouse, waiting downstairs.

Reflecting on this Oxford Group experience, Bill, in the first draft of the Twelve Steps, began Step Seven, "Humbly, on our knees . . . ." Ruth Hock tells of coming to work in 1936 for Bill and Hank P. at Hank's office on 17 William Street in Newark. Not clear on the nature of the business, she was astonished one day early in her employment to glimpse a visitor on his knees beside the desk in Hank and Bill's office, Hank and Bill hovering over him.

In 1935, after a summer of living with Bob and Anne, Bill returned to Brooklyn. He continued to attend Oxford Group meetings back in New York and to implement the ideas he and Dr. Bob had developed in Akron. Bill was single-minded in his concern for alcoholics and the application of Oxford Group principles to maintain sobriety, but he was not interested in the Oxford Group's zeal to save the world. In contrast, the Oxford Group, according to Buchman, was not interested in saving all the alcoholics in the world. Therefore, the alcoholics in New York came to a parting of the ways with the Oxford Group at Calvary Church in 1937. The Akron group split off from the Oxford Group two years later.

Bill and Bob kept in touch frequently by phone. Once a year, usually, Bob and Anne came east on their way to Vermont. They enjoyed a good visit with Bill and Lois in Bedford Hills. At least once a year, Bill and Lois, together with a car packed with New York-New Jersey members, headed for Akron for a similar get-together. (During the early and middle forties, because of gas shortages brought on by the war, not much individual traveling by car could be done.) And of course, a blessing for the archives, Bob and Bill corresponded often by letter. Some important letters from the late thirties and forties concern the book project, trustees of the Alcoholic Foundation and the Rockefeller people, royalties from the Big Book, structural plans of Bill's, anonymity, publicity, and the spread of the Fellowship.

Both Bob and Bill avoided power and position. This was one of their priceless gifts to A.A. Neither wanted to be regarded as a spiritual leader removed from a society of followers. Both rejected any attempt to put them on a pedestal. Each truly thought of himself as "just another drunk." And Bob, in his last address at the First International Convention of 1950, referred to his crucial role in the birth of A.A. as "possibly some small thing I did a number of years ago."

When Dr. Bob and Bill died, they were buried with the same humility they had shown in their lifetimes. Shortly before Dr. Bob's death, Akron A.A.s proposed to honor him with an imposing monument. When he showed the plans to Bill, he drawled, "I reckon we ought to be buried like other folks." Bill agreed emphatically. And so they were, both of them. Except for obituaries in the papers, in which their anonymity was broken, there was little fanfare. Their tombstones make no mention of A.A. Although memorial services were held by A.A.s throughout the nation and the world, only old friends and relatives attended their actual funeral and burial services.

The same care for personal privacy was observed at Lois' burial service on October 10, 1988, at East Dorset, Vermont, where she now rests beside Bill. This was equally true at Anne's service in June 1949 in Akron.

June 10, 1935, Bob's sobriety date, has been designated to mark the beginning of A.A. history and is celebrated as Founders' Day in Akron. But no other significant dates in their lives are celebrated or observed.

9

THE DECADES

Napoleon asked, "What is history but a fable generally agreed upon?" Tolstoy agreed that history is "a wonderful thing, if only it were true." As an old history teacher myself, I'm prejudiced. I find A.A. history fascinating. On those occasions when I have been privileged to talk about it before A.A. gatherings, I have sometimes tried to paint a broad-brush picture of the decades, something difficult to do because I like to share specific anecdotes and cite examples of what I describe. To me, each decade seems to have its own characteristics.

THE FORTIES—A SERIES OF FIRSTS

When the Big Book was published in April of 1939, there were only two groups (or "meetings" they were called then) and 100 members at most. There was not even a name for this "nameless bunch of drunks," as Bill described them. The period from 1935 to 1940 was mainly concerned with learning to get sober, with creating a textbook, and with creating a publishing and business office and a board of trustees for guidance.

The next year, 1940, was a year of impressive growth and many firsts. By year's end, 3,000 copies of the book had been sold. There were about 1,500 members, coast to coast, and about 50 groups. Some twelve or thirteen cities had quite stable groups by then. In addition to Akron and New York, these included Cleveland; Detroit; Greenwich, Connecticut; Philadelphia; Chicago; Los Angeles; Houston; Little Rock, Arkansas; Washington, D.C.; Richmond, Virginia; and St. Louis. An official office and the now-incorporated publishing side of A.A. was set up at 30 Vesey Street in downtown Manhattan for better access by visitors and because our official post office box was nearby.

Late in 1940, the first news bulletin was issued from the Vesey St. "headquarters" to the groups, and the first pamphlet, called simply A.A., was published. John D. Rockefeller, Jr., gave his famous dinner for A.A., the first clubhouse for members was opened in New York on Twenty-fourth Street, and the first A.A.-oriented drying-out facility, High Watch Farm in Kent, Connecticut, began operation. The custom of "passing the hat" at meetings to cover expenses was begun. Lots of good publicity appeared in newspapers and magazines, prompting some 2,000 inquiries to the office. Religious leaders began endorsing A.A. publicly. Father Edward Dowling, S.J., and Rev. Harry Emerson Fosdick were the first of many. Bill said later of the situation at the end of 1940: "The public began to be aware of us dimly . . . we could feel wonderful things to come." It was, he said, "sheer joy."

The Jack Alexander article in the *Saturday Evening Post* in March 1941 brought in a flood of inquiries—4,400 in just four months—and rapid growth. Membership went from 1,500 to 5,500 by the end of the year. The number of groups shot up to 170, and inquiries and letters came in from Canada, Africa, England, France, and Australia. Sales of the Big Book reached 3,600 copies for the year, and it went into a second printing. The Serenity Prayer, then called the A.A. Prayer, was adopted by the Fellowship, groups were asked to contribute one dollar per member twice a year to support the headquarters office, and as time went on there was increased publicity —books, movies, radio, newspapers, magazines, and documentaries by the March of Time and RKO Pathé.

One of my favorite people from the early days at the General Service Office was Al S. An advertising and film man in New York, Al reached his alcoholic bottom in March 1944 and called for help. He was put in touch with a member who took him to his first meeting at the old Twenty-fourth Street Clubhouse. He said he had an odd sense of well-being as he walked the long corridor—they called it "the last mile"—leading to the meeting room. Once inside, his old fears returned as he found himself surrounded by people talking about the Steps and the Program.

Within a month he was "into action," as the Big Book says. He helped re-form the Manhattan Group, whose roots reached back to the first meetings at Bill and Lois' house in Brooklyn in late 1935. He also helped organize another club for A.A.s on Forty-first Street and helped structure the New York Intergroup, for which he served as secretary and director. While there, he and another member, George B., were instrumental in persuading Knickerbocker Hospital to set aside a ward just for alcoholics under the sponsorship of A.A.—the first such general hospital in New York to do so.

"Those A.A.s had a job convincing us," the president of Knickerbocker recalled later. Among the obstacles was the fear that alcoholics would be unruly and would disturb the other patients, and the matter of financial responsibility. "But A.A. met each of these objections." It was, in fact, an example that other hospital programs followed. Al visited the ward at Knickerbocker every day to prevent problems from developing and to check on the progress of the patients. He became known for the prodigious amount of Twelfth Step work and sponsorship he continued to do throughout his life.

I first got to know Al when he was persuaded to become editor of the *Grapevine* in late 1948, succeeding Tom Y., its first editor. During the three-and-a-half years that Al was editor, he brought a new look to the *Grapevine* and opened its pages to a deeper and broader range of A.A. opinion and subject matter. In a letter to Bill in December 1949 he wrote: "Gradually we plan to shift the editorial emphasis away from the out-and-out 'drunk' stories and into stuff a bit more challenging. . . . Instead of beginning with the first drink, we begin with the last one. 'You're not drinking, now what?' 'How valuable is your sobriety to you?'" That remains the editorial thrust of the magazine.

Al had a good opportunity to put his ideas into practice, for in his early days on the *Grapevine* he wrote not only the editorials but nearly all the rest of the magazine as well, identifying each article with different initials. Later, however, the magazine came to be made up entirely of stories and articles contributed voluntarily and without pay by members throughout the country. Also during Al's tenure, Bill began to write more often for the *Grapevine*. Among the significant events chronicled during Al's editorship were the deaths of Anne S. on June 1, 1949, and Dr. Bob on November 16, 1950 (the memorial issue was in January 1951); the first International Convention of A.A. in Cleveland in 1950; and the first General Service Conference in April 1951.

During the time he was on the *Grapevine*, Al also served as a director of A.A. Publishing, Inc. (an earlier name of A.A. World Services, Inc.). And later on, he was very helpful in public affairs projects, like the DuPont "Cavalcade of America" program on A.A., which created a lot of interest. From 1958 to 1961, Al was a director of the A.A. Grapevine, Inc., and a trustee on the General Service Board.

Al attended, until his death, every international convention and contributed to them all. He composed the "I Am Responsible" pledge for the Toronto Convention and led the Sunday morning meeting in Denver. He also introduced Bill at his famous "Deep Freeze Talk" in Long Beach. Additionally at Long Beach, Al planned and produced a fine documentary film of the whole convention for the A.A. Archives, where it remains today. Although it is not available for general showing because of the anonymity tradition, it is a priceless and very moving historical record. Bill greatly valued Al's friendship, counsel, and wisdom. I know from my own experience that he solicited Al's views and comments on all his books and other writings. Lois put it succinctly: "Bill and Al were buddies."

Al also knew Dr. Bob and had an abiding admiration and affection for him as well. In fact, he drove Dr. Bob back home to Akron after the 1950 convention in Cleveland. He said later how intensely sad he felt on that journey as Bob was exhausted and in obvious pain.

I would describe those early years as a time of growing, learning, and maturing; of linking services that would promote ever more growth and stability for the Fellowship; of drawing on experience in developing the Twelve Traditions, especially the Tradition of self-support; and of facing and overcoming challenges and problems. When I came to the office in early 1947, I sensed the tremendous excitement of this decade.

THE FIFTIES—THE GENERAL SERVICE CONFERENCE BEGINS

The 1950s saw the beginning of the annual General Service Conference and Bill relinquish his overall guidance and responsibility for leadership to the groups. It was a time for putting the service structure into place and learning how to serve. It started with the first of the international conventions and the death of Dr. Bob. It went on to see some of Bill's most important writing and his proposals for meeting the needs of the growing Fellowship. World A.A. came into being and gained stability, and countries and geographical areas created their own service structure patterned after ours in the U.S. and Canada. At home, publicity in movies and television spurred further rapid growth. Al-Anon, guided by Lois and Anne B., grew rapidly, helped by the same guidelines and principles that served A.A. so well. Bill announced a writing program, which didn't materialize as planned, but which did come close: *The Twelve Steps and Twelve Traditions, Alcoholics Anonymous Comes of Age*, and the second edition of the Big Book.

THE SIXTIES—WORLDWIDE EXPANSION

The 1960s saw membership spread worldwide. More and better translations of A.A. literature were produced, service structures overseas were strengthened, and in 1969 the first of the biannual World Service Meetings was held.

In the U.S. and Canada, the decade brought closer encounters with the outside public. The first triannual survey of A.A. membership was conducted and the find-

90

ings were used to foster a better public understanding of A.A. The General Service Conference adopted Bill's "Twelve Concepts for World Service" and pamphlet of the same name, and the ratio on the General Service Board was changed to provide two-thirds A.A. members and one-third nonalcoholics. Bill retired from active participation. Dr. Jack Norris, summing up the decade, said it was a time for "exploring new concepts of service and new ways of carrying A.A.'s message."

The groundwork for this worldwide expansion had actually been laid by the first trip Bill and Lois took in 1950 to view A.A. in Europe. Even today I can vividly recall the excitement the trip generated among all of us back home, how eagerly we followed their progress and listened to them relate their adventures on their return.

A letter Bill wrote to Dr. Bob from Dublin reads, in part:

> We have been gone not quite seven weeks now and have visited four cities in Norway, three in Sweden, one in Denmark, two in Holland, as well as Paris, London, and now Dublin, Ireland. Lois and I both wish, Smithy, that you could have seen and felt what we have on this journey. We need not tell you that A.A. has come to Europe to stay. With its usual ease, it is breaking down all barriers of race, creed, language and tradition. Without much of any A.A. literature, a great job is being done, strongly reminiscent of our pioneering time at Akron, Cleveland and New York. Though they have the advantage of our background of success, the groups start here under very different circumstances than a new group starts up shop at home. Like us in the early days, they can take nothing for granted. The public still knows nothing about

them; the clergy and doctors, with a few exceptions, still wonder. The usual debates whether God made man, or man made God, rage on. They fear all sorts of calamities which you and I know won't happen, and yet they press on. It makes us relive old times.

The trip was a first step in creating service structures in the countries that were visited. I recall Bill writing a letter around 1954 to England recommending that they "consider creating a General Service Board of A.A. for England, Scotland and Ireland." Then he added: "We are anxious here that New York never be regarded as the world capital of A.A. . . . We want to be known as the senior service center of longest experience. . . ." That thinking was later incorporated into Bill's proposal, in 1968, for the World Service Meeting that took place in 1969.

Sadly, I also remember the sixties as a period when many notable figures in A.A. history were lost to us. I've already mentioned the passing of Fr. Ed Dowling and Sam Shoemaker, and in July 1965 we received a letter that Frank Amos had passed away. He was one of the Rockefeller people, one of the first trustees, who contributed so much to A.A. from 1937 on. In just over a week from the end of March to the first part of April in 1966, we lost three giants: Ebby T., Sister Ignatia, and Dr. Harry Tiebout.

THE SEVENTIES—MOVING ON WITHOUT THE COFOUNDERS

The 1970s began without the presence of either cofounder. There was, however, a firm commitment to go forward. Actually, thanks to the cofounders, the seventies was an era of unprecedented growth and health for the Fellowship. The passage of the Hughes Bill resulted in federal money being poured into alcoholism prevention and treatment, which brought A.A. further into the limelight and brought treatment center graduates in large numbers to A.A. meetings. The new interest in alcoholism led to Dr. Norris and others being invited to travel to other countries abroad to attend and speak to professional meetings.

Within A.A., miniconferences (soon renamed regional forums) brought better understanding of the board and the G.S.O. to service people throughout the U.S. and Canada. By the end of the decade, the Big Book would be selling in the millions of copies.

There was criticism, too. The Rand Report appeared, suggesting that A.A.'s emphasis on abstinence was "inaccurate," that it appeared *some* alcoholics could safely go back to drinking. After causing a noisy furor, the findings of this report were largely discredited and disappeared from view.

Special A.A. groups sprang up for young people, women, nonsmokers, the elderly, doctors, lawyers, airline pilots ("Birds of a Feather," they called themselves), and gay men and women. Outside A.A., scores of programs using the Twelve Steps were formed for those suffering from other illnesses or problems. From the standpoint of an archivist, I witnessed a great resurgence of interest in A.A. origins and history both within the Fellowship and by outsiders who used the A.A. Archives for doctoral theses, books, and articles.

THE EIGHTIES—WHAT HATH GOD WROUGHT!

I retired at the end of 1982, so a final perspective on the eighties is lacking. Suffice it to say that the growth and spread of Alcoholics Anonymous has continued at what is, to me and others, an incredible rate. A.A. is now flourishing in the Soviet Union, for example, as well as in Poland, Bulgaria, and Romania. It is estimated there are more than 87,000 groups in 134 countries around the globe, with an estimated membership in excess of 1.7 million, a bit different from the membership of 40,000 and 1,250 groups when I came in 1947. Sales of the Big Book in hardcover and softcover topped a million in one year in 1988. That's more than 5,000 every working day.

At the General Service Office in New York, A.A. World Services, plus the A.A. Grapevine, Inc., now occupies five floors. There are, all told, about 120 employees, including the *Grapevine* office. Surely Bill and Dr. Bob, looking down, are gratified that A.A. celebrated its fiftieth anniversary in 1985 intact and thriving worldwide. As Bill often exclaimed, "What hath God wrought!"

10

THE CONVENTIONS

Here's a little-known fact: Alcoholics Anonymous is by far the largest user of hotel rooms of any organization in the world. Conferences, conventions, round-ups, and other large gatherings abound in A.A. Most of these are sponsored by state, area, or regional service entities, but A.A. is so loosely organized that get-togethers may be put on by just about any member who has the urge, the energy, and the enthusiasm to do so. A.A.s flock to them. They enjoy being together, especially in large groups where the exuberance is contagious. One nonalcoholic friend of mine put it this way: "You have to understand, they would all be dead if it weren't for each other!" The G.S.O. calendar lists more than 300 major A.A. conferences and conventions in the U.S. and Canada every year, attended by 500 to 5,000 or more people. That's an average of a dozen or more every weekend. And that doesn't count similar gatherings in other countries.

Every five years, over a four-day July Fourth weekend, A.A. holds an international convention attended by members and their families from all over the world. The 1985 International Convention in Montreal, Canada, was attended by 45,000 people from 54 countries, and the 1990 Convention in Seattle recorded about 48,000 members from 75 countries. I have been at every international convention since 1955.

St. Louis, 1955

It's hard for people today to realize the enormity of the decision to accept a General Service Conference plan on that Sunday morning in St. Louis. Bill had pushed through the idea of such a conference largely by campaigning for it personally and relentlessly. Many members, particularly in the Midwest, still opposed the idea, and several of us in the audience knew that one of them, a controversial and influential priest, who opposed Bill's turning over his leadership, had threatened to rise and speak against it.

After Bill presented his resolution, Bernard Smith, the chairman, asked for a moment of silence for the crowd to invoke the guidance of God. I sat there with baited breath. But there was only hushed silence. Then Bern called for the vote and a roar of approval went up. Tears came to my eyes. I was sitting with Dennis Manders, then the nonalcoholic supervisor of the accounting department, and emotion filled him, too. He and I watched as Bill, to dramatize the fact that he was stepping down, physically stepped down from the stage in Kiel Auditorium. A.A. had come of age. It was standing on its own now, a self-governing body organized around the conference, not the cofounder.

Dennis liked to kid about it years later, saying "It took Bill 12 more years to take the last step." And it was true that Bill continued his custom of spending a day or two a week at the General Service Office, often answering mail, and he was certainly involved with the trustee ratio dispute and many other issues until the late sixties. He continued to play a prominent part in the general service conferences and international conventions during those years, as well as being involved in the preparation for the first World Service Meeting in 1969, at which time his health was failing badly. But after 1955 he was freed from the day-to-day concerns of the office. Incidentally, most of his decade-long depression lifted following the St. Louis convention; he pretty much regained his bright outlook on life.

Aside from the thrill of this momentous step in A.A. history, my other memory of St. Louis is of the oppressive heat. It must have been over 100 degrees with heavy humidity. We had to change clothes several times a day just to stay looking fresh. Bill and Lois were exhausted from the lack of sleep and emotional strain.

So many figures who were important to A.A.'s formative years were present in St. Louis, and their talks are reprinted in *Alcoholics Anonymous Comes of Age*. They include Fr. Edward Dowling, S.J.; Rev. Samuel Shoemaker; Dr. W.W. Bauer of the American Medical Association; and Bernard Smith, at that time chairman of the General Service Board. Dr. Harry Tiebout came all the way from Greenwich, CT, to be in St. Louis.

Bill once said that it was from Shoemaker, the Episcopal clergyman active in the New York Oxford Group during the twenties and thirties, that he observed most of the principles that were embodied in the Twelve Steps. He once wrote, "Sam passed on the spiritual keys by which we were liberated." Shoemaker was charismatic—a tall, handsome, friendly man, a little portly, with a strong voice. He gave a marvelous talk in St. Louis.

Dr. Leonard Strong couldn't make it to St. Louis, which disappointed Bill. Dr. Strong was Bill's brother-in-law, and was married to Bill's sister, Dorothy. When almost everyone else had deserted Bill and Lois, Leonard saw them through the worst of Bill's drinking. Later he was the absolutely essential link between Bill and the people around John D. Rockefeller, Jr., through his old friend Rev. Willard Richardson, who handled Mr. Rockefeller's private charities. This connection led directly to the formation of the Alcoholic Foundation. It is no exaggeration to say that without him, there would have been no A.A., or at least the history would have been vastly different. One of so many nonalcoholics who made a difference in A.A.'s beginnings, Dr. Strong died on April 24, 1989.

Bernard Smith was chairman of the convention and was chairman of the General Service board at that time. When Bill was trying to push through the idea of the conference, Bern Smith was the only trustee—or, anybody— supporting him, and it was he who finally brought a majority of the other trustees around to accept the conference on a trial basis. He also helped Bill put together the proposed General Service Conference structure; Bill called him "the architect of the conference." Stocky in build, quick of wit and mind, perceptive, he also relished a few drinks. He sometimes referred to himself as a "*so-called* nonalcoholic." He was devoted to Bill and to A.A. until his untimely death a month after substituting for Bill at the 35th Anniversary Convention in Miami.

Ebby T. was in St. Louis as Bill's special guest, brought up from Texas, where he had moved the year before with the assistance of several New York and Texas members. This was about the time that Ebby started to look after an alcoholic young woman who eventually died, leaving him distraught and causing him to slip and return to New York in the early sixties. His six years of sobriety in Texas proved to be his longest sober period. Bill and Lois tried to care for him again for a while, but he continued to slip. However, he died sober in March 1966, thanks to having spent the last two years of his life at Margaret and Mickey McP.'s rest farm at Ballston Spa, near Schenectady, New York.

Another special guest in St. Louis was Bill's mother, Dr. Emily Strobell. She had divorced his father and left Bill with her parents when he was eleven years old, and Bill seemed desperate to seek his mother's approval all his life. Though not on a regular basis, he did see his mother from time to time and they corresponded frequently. He particularly wanted to have her with him at this special convention to hear him speak and see how the members and friends reacted to his contributions. Bill said it was "the icing on the cake" for him.

One of my principal duties at the convention was to keep Dr. Emily company during the day when Bill and Lois were busy elsewhere at meetings and special events. I always felt she closely resembled my grandmother: patrician in appearance and style, elegant and handsome, but a bit formidable. She was a doctor of osteopathy living then in San Diego. (Her second husband, Dr. Charles Strobell, died, I believe, in 1936.)

Bill often referred to his mother as "Hetty" after the famous Hetty Green, who in the early part of the century amassed a large fortune and wielded an equally large amount of political power. The reference here is to the fact that Dr. Emily had, at about age 75, turned her attention to the stock market where she discovered she had quite a talent for knowing just when to buy and sell. In her very late years, Bill had brought her east, and for a year or two she lived with Bill and Lois at Stepping Stones. Going up on weekends, I would go into her bedroom to say good-night in the evening, and I was always amused and amazed at what became a familiar sight—seeing her sitting up in bed, knees up, eyeglasses on, poring over the latest stock market reports.

At the convention, I didn't see how Dr. Emily could have helped but be impressed with her son, but she didn't show too much reaction one way or the other. When members would express their gratitude for Bill's impact on their lives, she would quickly remind them that *they* too affected people's lives. Later, living with Bill and Lois, she expressed deep devotion and appreciation to visitors and their friends for Bill's contributions to A.A. She liked his A.A. friends, and we enjoyed a friendship over those last years until her passing.

Occasionally, she sent short notes, which she signed, "Heap-Big-Love, Bill's 'Mom' " revealing her sense of humor and fun. I would like to share just a few lines from a couple of letters:

> Dear Nell Wing: You made it snappy, didn't you [referring to a quick thank-you note]. Well, you are a pretty snappy gal anyway you put it; even your name makes you a one-syllable gal . . . glad you got the pecans OK. There are a lot of nuts in the world, as is, but they are mostly already cracked, making the pecans the best nuts going, don't you think? . . . nonsensically yours . . .

Again:

> Dear Nell Wing: Thank you so very much for remembering me at Christmas time with the beautiful card. I miss you very much. . . .

And a last message before she died:

> Dear Nell: Thank you for remembering me with that pretty card, and note. You were always thoughtful and kind. Do you remember

100

the hilarious laughs we used to have at Lois',
with you sitting on the edge of the bed? I do.
. . . Love to you, Bill's Mom.
She died on May 15, 1961.

As always, Lois contributed her ideas, enthusiasm, and
energy to the St. Louis Convention—concentrating on her
Al-Anon Family Groups, but also active throughout. On
the Sunday afternoon of the closing "coming of age" part
of the program, she was the first speaker to address the
crowd in Kiel Auditorium after the vote to turn over leadership to the Fellowship had been taken.

LONG BEACH, 1960

The 1960 Convention was held in Long Beach, California.
Hank G., manager of the General Service Office, was
supervising this convention also. He decided on his way to
California with his new wife to stop for a few days in Las
Vegas. While there, he was stricken with appendicitis and
ended up in a hospital. Herb M., the chairman of the
trustees' General Services Committee, was probably the
next most knowledgeable person, but he was suddenly
stricken with a heart attack in upstate New York. So at the
very last moment, Allen B., another trustee, had to step
into the breach and take charge of the convention with
almost no preparation. Fortunately Allen was a good
administrator, extremely capable and well-liked. Al S.
assisted him. Allen, Dennis Manders, staff secretary
Hazel R., and Bill went out to California several days
ahead to get started.

Lois and I followed on the already scheduled flight.
When we landed, we were met by members of the hospitality committee. After greeting us, they continued to wait
around until Lois asked if we were ready to leave. They

101

replied, "We're waiting for Bill's Chinese secretary." Lois laughed and said, "This is Nell Wing right here," pointing to my decidedly Caucasian features. I'll always remember that one.

There were twice as many people at Long Beach as at St. Louis. Bill planned (following the usual program at these conventions) to make a major talk on Saturday night. He wanted it to be the definitive story of the how and why of the Twelve Traditions. But because of the many distractions resulting from Hank's illness, Bill hadn't had the time to prepare for this important talk. I spent the whole day Saturday with him going over and over the outline and notes for the speech. I typed and retyped them as he changed and added. Finally, we left for the open-air stadium right on the ocean where the huge crowd had gathered.

Not a soul who was there will ever forget it, for two reasons. First, a record cold spell came in. Nobody had brought any warm clothes, of course, so, in contrast to St. Louis where we almost melted, here we almost froze. Second, Bill went on and on for more than two hours. It was the longest talk he ever made. To make matters worse, the public address system was set up so that Lois and the trustees, who were seated on the stage behind the podium, couldn't hear a word for the entire two hours. The old-timers who were there often chuckled later about Bill's "Deep Freeze Talk"—as he himself first described it. Amazingly, almost everyone stayed until the end, shivering and shaking.

Sunday, in the same stadium, the Los Angeles A.A.s had arranged a spectacular show featuring a popular orchestra and some of Hollywood's brightest stars including Buster Keaton, Jayne Mansfield, Dennis Day, and Peggy Lee—all of whom donated their talent without charge. Clancy I., sitting with us up front in the audience, bundled himself with newspapers inside his clothes like a wino and attracted almost as much attention as the performers. Bill B., an entertainer who was the MC, kidded Bill lovingly about the length of the talk. Bill laughed, too, and took it all in good humor.

TORONTO, 1965

The 30th Anniversary Convention in Toronto, Canada, was the first held outside the U.S. I have a soft spot in my heart to this day for those wonderful, warm Canadians who simply couldn't do enough for us. Bill and Lois were prominent on the program, as usual, and at that time, lots of old-timers were still active and at the convention.

I particularly remember Clarence S., with whom Bill spent a couple of hours in his hotel suite reminiscing about the early days. Clarence was the first person to break away from the Akron meeting, which was sharing space with the Oxford Group meeting in the home of T. Henry Williams. He started a group in Cleveland in May 1939, the first group, as far as we know, to use the A.A. initials. (Bill had been using the full name since 1938 in letters and a pamphlet.) On this slender basis, Clarence forever claimed to have founded A.A.

As long as Bill was alive, Clarence was antagonistic and hostile toward him. He was a leader of a small group of dissidents, who were anti-Conference and anti-G.S.O. and who bad-mouthed Bill for many years. And here was Bill in Toronto, chatting and chuckling with his bête noire and enjoying it all. I believe that was the last time they met together.

The feisty priest who had threatened to disrupt the "Coming of Age" ceremony in St. Louis, was at this convention also, but now he was loving and kind to Bill and Lois and everyone else. He had just returned from an audience with the Pope in Rome, bearing a citation for Bill. It hangs now on the wall at Stepping Stones.

The film *Bill's Own Story*, which I had watched being made at Stepping Stones, was shown for the first time in Toronto. It was well received and has been reproduced in several languages since then.

As I mentioned, Al S. composed the "I Am Responsible" pledge for the occasion. I will never forget—nor will anyone who was there—the moving ceremony of rededication on Saturday evening in the Maple Leaf Gardens auditorium. The crowd of more than 10,000 rose and joined the conference delegates, trustees, and A.A. representatives from 21 countries up on the stage in repeating the declaration. They clasped hands and loudly pronounced in one tremendous, strong voice:

I am responsible. When anyone, anywhere reaches out for help, I want the hand of A.A. always to be there. And for that: I am responsible.

There was a special spirit about the Toronto Convention. Many people say it was the best ever.

MIAMI BEACH, 1970

The largest gathering of A.A. and Al-Anon to date was held in July 1970 at the Fountainbleu and Eden Roc hotels in Miami Beach. More than 13,000 members and their families came from all over the world to see the cofounder and hear him speak, as he had at all previous conventions, and to participate in the wide-ranging program.

But Bill was much too sick. His lifelong cigarette habit had caught up with him in the form of emphysema, even though he had given up smoking the year before. In early spring 1969, while working up on the slate roof of his studio at Stepping Stones, he fell. He grabbed a tree branch, which helped break the fall, but he stubbornly returned to the roof to finish the job. That was the beginning of the end. He never fully recovered from the effects of the fall, and his health began to deteriorate more rapidly. The next year saw more decline. That April at A.A.'s annual General Service Conference, he was unable to finish his opening talk, to the shock and consternation of the delegates and trustees present.

I flew down with Bill and Lois to the Miami convention a few days early. At these gatherings, I stayed pretty much at Bill's side to help with his notes for his talks. This time, it was clear that Bill wasn't up to his scheduled appearances. The usual press conference was held the Wednesday afternoon before the weekend conference began. Marty M. and Dr. Jack Norris filled in for Bill, I remember, and Lois was present, of course.

Once or twice a day, we had to take Bill back and forth to the Miami Health Clinic. Lois, Bob H., general manager of A.A.'s General Service Office, and Dr. Jack were spread pretty thin trying to cope, trying to keep the huge convention going and easing anxiety caused by Bill's failure to appear. I was caring for Bill in their suite upstairs at the hotel. It was during that week that he began hallucinating, imagining he had made a long-distance call. It was terribly distressing for Lois. I remember Lois' courage and determination to "carry on" with Al-Anon's participation in the convention. It seems to me that Al-Anon more than ever "came of age" on this occasion, with its own program of events and big crowds in its own headquarters hotel, the Eden Roc, next to the Fountainbleu where the A.A.s were meeting.

I was surprised and thrilled at the number of foreign-speaking members from overseas, especially from Latin America. It was a truly international gathering.

A.A.s consume an unbelievable amount of coffee at these conventions. The host committee in Miami, chaired by Wes P., one of the more colorful members, had raised some $10,000 from local groups to provide complimentary coffee, served from a hospitality station in the lobby and in their hospitality suite. Well, $10,000 worth of coffee (at hotel prices) had been consumed before the afternoon was over on the first day of the convention, and the coffee kitty was empty.

Bernard Smith, the past chairman of the General Service Board and a good friend of Bill's, was called down from New York to deliver the main speech that Saturday night, in Bill's place. He was a little disgruntled at the short notice and asked me to help him adapt a talk from a previous conference, which I did.

I recall we finished up Saturday about one or two o'clock, whereupon he left to play a little golf. On Sunday, when I saw him in the hotel lobby, he came over to apologize for his irritability the day before.

I was so exhausted by Saturday night that I slept in on Sunday morning and missed the program. During the huge closing meeting that morning, Bill put in a surprise appearance. They wheeled him in from the back of the stage, hooked up with tubes to an oxygen tank, and clad, at his own insistence, in one of the orange-colored blazers that identified the Miami host committee. I understand the whole hall simply exploded into applause. As the noise subsided, I was told, he heaved himself up from the wheelchair, to his full height, hands on the rostrum. He spoke for perhaps five minutes, his voice clear and strong, the old Bill at his best. He spoke of how impressed he was with the large attendance, particularly the members from

106

other countries. He mentioned what it had meant to him to see A.A.'s enormous growth and to have been a part of it. And he ended with a few moving words that will never be forgotten by the thousands who heard them: "As I look out this morning on this vast crowd, I know in my heart that Alcoholics Anonymous will surely last a thousand years—if it is God's will!" As he sat down in his wheelchair, the audience rose in a tumultuous ovation. Thus I missed one of the most meaningful and moving appearances he ever made before A.A. Many times since I've thought about the coincidence, the similarity of the final exit of the two cofounders twenty years apart.

Later that day, I went back to New York. Bill returned to the hospital with Lois. They remained in Miami until August, when the decision was made to return home to Stepping Stones. Hardly had they done so when Bill's condition took another downturn. He began to require oxygen constantly and his hallucinations were getting worse. Bill first had one nurse; in a couple of months, two more nurses were added round the clock. By this time, I was coming up to Stepping Stones more often. As I said before, in mid-January of 1971 my own mother had died, and I had just returned to Stepping Stones to try to recover from her death when Bill's health went into its final, fatal decline.

DENVER, 1975

In Denver, Bill was no longer with us. The platform of Currigan Hall was decorated with portraits of Bill and Dr. Bob and a 30-foot replica of the Big Book between them. Lois was very active, as usual, with the Al-Anon program. On Sunday morning, Al S. led the huge "spiritual meeting" and Lois gave a very moving talk.

My predominant impression of the Denver convention was crowds, crowds, crowds. The General Service Office had planned for 12,000 and about 20,000 showed up. The workshops and panel meeting rooms were hopelessly jammed, and at the big meetings the crowds overflowed Currigan Hall into a sports arena across the street where the talks were carried on a closed-circuit TV screen. In fact, I remember the fire department was a bit alarmed at the overcrowding of the halls.

My role was different in 1975. Now I attended not as Bill's assistant but as the A.A. archivist, working alongside George G., chairman of the Trustees' Archives Committee. George still serves as a consultant to the Trustees' Archives Committee. I'm so grateful for his contributions to the organizing and supervision in the earliest days of the archives, and for his friendship personally.

In Denver, he and I lined up a number of early members, and we spent most of our time interviewing them to get their oral histories on tape. It was a wonderful, heart-warming experience for me, because I had kept up with these old-timers by mail.

Also in Denver, an entrepreneur who had heard of the prodigious amount of coffee consumed at A.A. conventions rigged the world's largest coffee maker with servers on both sides of the balcony at the convention hall. It had a capacity of 500,000 cups a day. The coffee was brewed in huge tanks or vats and piped to a bank of dozens of spigots where we helped ourselves after paying a quarter a cup. It worked fine and was the talk of the convention, but the coffee itself—well, I've tasted better!

The emotional high point of the convention was the flag ceremony that preceded the formal opening Friday night. As spotlights played, the name of each country represented was called over the public address system. To the strains of music from that country, its flag was carried down the aisle and onto the stage. A.A.s from 29 nations paraded their flags. Each flag bearer stepped up to the microphone on the stage and repeated the conference theme, "Let It Begin With Me," in his or her native tongue. The flag ceremony, which had been conceived by office manager Kleina Jones of G.S.O., was such a resounding success that it would become a fixture of future international conventions.

NEW ORLEANS, 1980

In 1980 in New Orleans, it was terribly hot and humid. This was the 45th Anniversary International Convention. The big meetings were held in the immense, air-conditioned Superdome, which was comfortably chilled and acoustically perfect. There was a mock Mardi Gras parade on Thursday night. Famed Bourbon Street turned into "ice-cream and coffee" street as mobs of A.A.s overran it. Signs in the windows of the jazz joints welcomed us. Behind the stage at the Friday night opening was a 30-foot-high world map outlined on a blue background. During the flag ceremony, as each flag bearer spoke the theme, "Joy of Living," in his or her native language, lights began to twinkle on the map.

We held our first archives workshop at an international convention and the attendance was large and enthusiastic. As I mentioned, we had just completed producing a filmstrip of the archives entitled *Markings on a Journey*, which we showed continuously throughout the convention along with the films *Bill's Own Story* and *Bill Discusses the Traditions*. That was exciting for me and all of us involved with the archives. Mike R., a pioneer member from Oklahoma who was also a chairman of the

Trustees' Archives Committee and a devoted supporter of and contributor to the archives, loved the fact that some 2,000 members visited the archives in New York annually just to heighten their awareness of "where it all began" and to see the memorabilia. But Mike felt that since it was impossible to bring all the Fellowship in to see the archives, we should in some way take the archives to the Fellowship. *Markings on a Journey* was our attempt to do just that. We also scheduled a meeting of area and state archivists after the workshop and discussed the value of circulating a newsletter among our archivists.

There were other historic moments at the New Orleans Convention. It was the first to recognize gay alcoholics with their own program. It was the first to have a "marathon meeting" that ran continuously, day and night, from Thursday midnight to Sunday morning. A man who had sobered up just two days before in the marathon meeting was introduced before the crowd of 23,000. On Sunday morning, Lois was introduced for a brief talk. She was presented with the first Big Book in the Italian language. Roberto C., the warm and charming man who had done the translation, made the presentation and told us how A.A. was growing in Italy.

Next, a surprise guest came to the microphone. He introduced himself as Bob S., a member of Al-Anon, and you could almost feel the questioning from the crowd. Then he explained that he was probably the only person there who had been present when Bill W. met Dr. Bob, because he was the only son of Dr. Bob S. Pandemonium broke out in the Superdome, people standing and applauding with tears streaming down their faces. He went on to share some of his early memories of Bill's living in their Akron home that summer in 1935, and he continues today to do just that. He and his lovely wife

110

Betty are dearly loved by all A.A.s, Al-Anons, and friends.

MONTREAL, 1985

For me, the most exciting of all the international conventions was the 50th Anniversary Convention in Montreal in 1985. It drew 45,000 members and their families. Because the emphasis of the whole event was Alcoholics Anonymous history, but mostly, I think, because I was accompanying Lois, I was on the platform in the middle of the vast Olympic Stadium Friday night for the opening ceremonies. They began with the flag ceremony with 54 countries represented. It was a fantastic sight viewed from the platform, with the audience appearing far in the distance.

Lois, a tiny, stooped figure now at age 94, was assisted by her secretary, Francis H., to the microphone, where she delivered a short but touching speech in a strong voice with her sense of humor evident. Ruth Hock was presented with the five-millionth copy of the Big Book, the original manuscript of which she had typed in 1938. Ruth had been Bill's first secretary from 1936 to 1942. She typed and retyped the first manuscript of the Big Book, with Bill standing behind her dictating as she typed; afterward, she helped settle the squabbles among the members about the book's content. She was much more than a gifted secretary, she was a major factor in the stability and functioning of that early office. In fact, she was a balancing factor in the debate between Jim B., the former atheist, and Fitz M., who was strongly religious, that resulted in the use of the phrase *God as we understood Him* in the Steps—certainly one of the most significant decisions ever made in A.A. What would later be called the "Serenity Prayer" was brought to her attention in June 1941. She sent it to an A.A. member (who was a printer) in Washington, D.C., and he printed it on small cards for distribution from G.S.O. to interested members. We became friends and remained so until her death in the spring of 1986.

Dave B., the founder of A.A. in Montreal, was to have been honored also, but he had died only a few weeks before and was represented by nonalcoholic past trustee Dr. Travis Dancey, who had first tried to bring the A.A. message to Dave. Chairman Emeriti Dr. Jack Norris and Dr. Milton Maxwell, and Dr. Bob's son and daughter, Bob S. and Sue Windows, and Bob's wife Betty were there. Dennis Manders also attended as did 89-year-old Ken S., a "long-timer" from Kansas City. One of the talks that night was given by Sybil C., the first woman member in Los Angeles and at this time, the woman with the longest sobriety (44 years) in A.A.

We held an archives workshop in Montreal organized by Frank M., the present archivist, and we also had old-timers' meetings and pioneers' meetings. The closing talk in the Olympic Stadium Sunday morning was by Joe McQ., the first black member in Little Rock, Arkansas, in 1962. Over several years, in partnership with Charlie P., he participates in Big Book seminar sessions held frequently all around the country, Canada, and overseas. His was a stirring and moving story.

SEATTLE, 1990

During this convention I felt more deeply aware than ever before of the uplifting spirit, the warmth, and the sense of unity that radiated at all events and activities. Even though this was the largest-yet A.A. gathering, the warm and sincere welcome extended to all of us by the Seattle citizens, taxi drivers, shopkeepers, etc., made it feel as personal as all the others. (In 1965, at the 30th Anniversary Convention in Toronto, I remember an example of a considerate gesture on the part of the bartender in the hotel bar. One of our nonalcoholic trustees decided he would like a drink, went into the bar, sat down, ordered and was surprised when the bartender refused to serve him. The reason was soon discovered—he had *forgotten* he was wearing his convention A.A. badge!)

The spontaneity of this welcome was all the more remarkable considering the large number of A.A. and Al-Anon members inundating the city and facilities: the official count was 48,000, and 75 countries were represented. As always, the opening (Friday) night flag ceremony was a high point. The hall really let go when the Soviet, Bulgarian, and Romanian flags were carried to the front of the platform. Dr. Bob's son and daughter, Bob. S. and Sue Windows, and Bob's wife Betty were also on hand to witness the event.

It was also a homecoming of sorts for me. I had spent 1944-46 in Seattle (the 13th naval district) as a member of SPARS, the Women's Coast Guard Reserve. In the basement of the Olympic Hotel (now affiliated with the Four Seasons chain) there was a large bar and dining room which we called the "snake pit" and where many of us, along with Coast Guard and Navy guys did a bit of off-duty drinking. One night I got involved in an all-night drinking spree and next morning, up before my executive officer, was "awarded" a captain's mast and sentenced to a brief confinement in my quarters (the "brig" was full). I was allowed out once a day, accompanied by a shore patrol.

Now, 44 years later, here I was in Seattle again and the recipient of the 10 millionth copy of the Big Book. No words can adequately express my deep gratitude to this beloved Fellowship and my cherished friends therein.

11

LAUGHTER IS THE BEST MEDICINE

I don't know if anyone has written adequately about the role of humor and laughter in Alcoholics Anonymous. For me, it was one of the most surprising features of the Fellowship in the early days of my service. Like most people, I suppose I had imagined A.A. meetings to be rather grim, but nothing could be further from the truth. There is probably more spontaneous laughter at A.A. meetings than at any other kind of meeting I can think of.

I remember about a month after I started working at the Foundation, I was asked if I'd like to attend one of the monthly, city-wide open A.A. meetings at the Engineers Hall on Forty-first Street. This monthly Friday night meeting featured nonalcoholic friends of A.A., like Rev. Sam Shoemaker and Fr. Ed Dowling, when he was in town, and of course, talks by Bill, Marty, and one or two local members. This particular evening, I think Sam Shoemaker was the main speaker, and it was also the first time I had heard Bill or Marty speak. There was a long-time New York member who shared his story also. Listening to him tell about the drinking episodes, how he recovered and what life was like now, brought tears to my eyes. But during the telling, suddenly, all around me, I was aware of waves of laughter breaking out intermittently. Not only was I puzzled but a little angry. Here was this poor soul, describing what I considered tragic episodes in his life, and yet everyone was laughing hilariously. It seemed so impolite, I thought, at the time.

But I was soon to learn that laughter in A.A. is not a superficial, polite action. It is a healing, life-saving force, a special part of the A.A. lifeline, an instantaneous gut-level recognition and identification with the speaker that says, "Yes, I was that bad, too. We were terrible, weren't we. But now we're okay." Whatever triggers the laughter is an in-joke that is almost impossible to capture or explain, but let me share a few stories.

A speaker tells of criss-crossing the country in boxcars, not caring where he was headed or where he was, not caring whether he turned right or turned left. He adds brightly, "I was never lost!" (Gales of laughter) Another speaker confesses that when he drank he was a terrible liar.

> I lied to my wife about where I'd been and what I'd been doing, I lied to my boss about why I failed to show up, and I finally got so I lied just out of habit, even when there was no reason to lie. (Sympathetic laughter)

Clancy I. was brilliant and successful in advertising, a career he gave up to run the Midnight Mission in the skid row area of Los Angeles. In his A.A. talk, he often tells of being incarcerated as an alcoholic in the Texas state insane asylum at Big Springs. He slyly plotted and planned and finally made his escape. But outside the asylum, stretching to the farthest horizon, there was nothing but the parched

116

plains of West Texas, not a house nor a tree nor a road. "The guards didn't even come after me," relates Clancy. "They just watched me running out into that vast empty plain in my paper slippers and pajamas with my bathrobe flapping behind me, and drawled to each other, 'W-a-a-ll, that'n'll be back.' "

The A.A. Grapevine, the monthly journal of the Fellowship, contains innumerable examples of the kind of humor that A.A.s instantly recognize. For example:

> Many of you probably heard Frank Fontaine, on the Jackie Gleason Show, tell about his drunken relatives who, he said, started A.A.
>
> "You mean they founded A.A.?" asked Gleason.
>
> "No," said Fontaine, "they were the cause of it."[17]

Or this:

> Tuesday night featured a long-winded speaker. After forty minutes, he had hardly gotten past World War II. He paused to catch his breath. Clearly, everyone heard a listener say to his neighbor, "I wonder what comes next."
>
> And everyone heard the reply: "Wednesday."[18]

Or a cartoon I particularly like because it plays on A.A.'s First Step (". . . admitted we were powerless over alcohol"), Twelfth Step (". . . tried to carry this message to alcoholics . . ."), and the active alcoholic's denial of his problem. The cartoon shows a drunk sprawled in the gutter with a concerned, well-dressed man bending over him. The drunk is saying, "I'm not powerless over alcohol, I just can't get up."[19]

A.A. members' attitudes toward humor were well expressed on a printed card that was circulated widely back in the forties. On the front it read, "Rule No. 62."

When you turned it over, it read "Don't take yourself too damned seriously."

The archives are also full of humor about A.A. and some of the early clippings refer to the confusion between the initials A.A. and AAA in the forties. A cartoon from the British magazine *Punch* shows two spectators standing beside a smashed car, the loser in a contest with a lamp post. One of the onlookers, noticing the "smashed" but unhurt condition of the driver, says to his friend, "What should we call first—the AAA or A.A.?" Then there's the story of the problem drinker who says he has joined the AAA. His friend asks him, "Don't you mean A.A.?" and the drunk replies, "No, I mean AAA. When I'm drinking I have to be towed away from the bar."

There's a political cartoon from 1963 by Bill Mauldin picturing world leaders Jack Kennedy, Harold Macmillan, and Nikita Khrushchev sitting at a conference table under a wall sign reading, "Charter Meeting of Megatons Anonymous." The caption underneath the cartoon reads, "Anyone who feels himself slipping should call one of the others."

Occasionally, popular comic strips have carried an A.A. story line. The first I remember was back in 1949 when the creator of a widely syndicated strip called "Wash Tubbs" used an A.A. story for several weeks. All of us in the office were terribly excited about this publicity. Later "Mary Worth" did a fine job portraying an A.A. situation. At one time, "Pogo" proposed a new group, "Unknowns Anonymous." You had to be a "confirmed nobody" to qualify. The popular "B.C." carried a proposal to form "Losers Anonymous." Today, of course, there are hundreds of important "anonymous" organizations patterned after A.A.

Lots of A.A. wisdom carries a "zinger." From a member in Glendale, California: "Our goal in A.A. is not to be better than someone else, but to be better than ourselves." A member from Tampa observed, "A.A. is like a log floating downstream. On this log there are a million ants clinging to it—and each one thinks he's steering."

There are a couple of true stories I particularly like. One of them concerns a woman who called one of the A.A. intergroup offices, just furious, asking, "*When* are you people ever going to have an opening? My husband has told me for months that he's still on the waiting list!"

The other story is in a similar vein. It is about Tom B., who at the bottom of his drinking career back in the forties, was told by his wife to contact A.A.—or else! Crafty Tom agreed to do so but a devious plan was forming in his alcoholic mind. He would keep his promise, which did not include *where* to contact A.A. So Tom promptly wrote a letter, thus getting his wife off his back, and posted it to as far away as he could think of: "Alcoholics Anonymous, Capetown, South Africa." To his utter dismay, a few weeks later he received a warm, welcoming letter from the A.A. group in Capetown, saying how glad they were that he had made his decision. Tom was so unnerved he gave in to his fate and accepted the Capetown, South Africa, group as his sponsor. Eventually he started a group in his city that he named the "Capetown II group" and, as far as I know, it's still in existence.

Bill once remarked, "Without a real sense of humor, A.A. could not exist at all."

Finally, I don't know whether it was because Bill W. and Dr. Bob were Vermonters or because of the era in which they grew up, but both of them used amusing expressions. For example, when Bill was ready to take a walk with Lois and me, he'd say, "Let's take a tunk." I can't imagine where that one came from, nor could Lois. When a debate or an argument was coming to a climax, it was "hotting up." I've

already mentioned one of his favorite sayings, "Hold fast"
—meaning stay with it, hang in there, and there was "pass
it on" to those who tried to thank him for their sobriety. If
he wasn't feeling up to par, he was "cooking up soggy."

The turbulent early days of A.A. had their share of
setbacks and disappointments, of course. On hearing of
disagreements in groups or between people, Bill would say
in a mock rural Vermont accent, "(H)it's the people!" Or a
variation on that if, for example, a member had a slip:
"Oh, the people, they won't stay fixed." Or if someone
broke his anonymity or a squabble broke out in a clubhouse, Bill would say, "That's life among the anonymii."

12

PRESERVING THE EXPERIENCE

During my last ten years at the General Service Office, I served as the archivist for Alcoholics Anonymous. This was one of the richest and most fulfilling periods of my life. The position required some professional knowledge, a lot of creativity, and an overview of A.A. history, particularly people, places, and events.

Although I wasn't given the title of archivist until 1972, I began archival activity about 1957. As I mentioned before, in 1954, Bill planned for a "writing and research team" consisting of himself, Ed B., and me. But because of Bill's still bothersome depressions, the writing project didn't get off the ground. We did manage to do the second edition of the Big Book. But then Ed and I were left at 305 East Forty-fifth Street, with all the old, early files and records of the groups and office, which had been brought out of storage and placed in the adjoining room. Bill admonished me, "Now, Nell, you and Ed give what time you can to getting all this stuff in order. It's got to be sorted out and then preserved."

Bill later explained that the reason for his intense interest in preserving the history records was to ensure that "the basic facts of A.A.'s growth and development never can become distorted." By the mid-fifties, he realized that the facts were already being distorted by some. Also Bill saw the sweep and scope of the Fellowship he had cofounded, and foresaw its significance as a social movement to be studied by future historians, scholars, and researchers. His awareness of this started in the late thirties, when he reminded Lois to begin preserving newspaper and magazine articles and letters, which she did enthusiastically.

So, in our small quarters at 305 East Forty-fifth, Ed and I began wading through the old group files and office files. For lunch, Ed and I often walked to the wonderful Tudor Hotel restaurant on East Forty-second Street. The waiter, finding that Ed couldn't speak because of his laryngectomy, thought he was deaf also. So he would repeat our order in a loud voice, speaking very slowly, as if we were mentally slow as well, which caused Ed to bristle and squirm angrily in his seat.

Ed and I worked comfortably together as we began to review the letters and reports, except that Ed favored discarding about 90 percent of them as "not important" enough to preserve. I, on the other hand, wanted to preserve 90 percent! Rather than get into arguments, after Ed left each afternoon, I rescued the letters he had consigned to the wastebasket. A large amount of early A.A. history was thus retrieved from the trash can.

Until the last few decades, the word *archives* was not in general use except in connection with historical museums or private collections. When Bill assigned us this task, I looked for books on the subject, but found little except one on indexing and cataloguing, which I was already familiar with.

In 1955, I also visited several places in the city I thought would have archival setups, but found little of benefit. At the New York Public Library, for example, they took me down to the cellar where there were rows and rows of letter boxes full of material they considered worth preserving but they told me I would have to devise my own system. It was dark and dreary down there and I was happy to leave. It was the same elsewhere. I found little experience or advice I could use—just "do it yourself, and good luck."

One day I read of a new "Records Management" service on Forty-second Street. Thinking, "At last! Help is at hand!" I hurried over. Two or three men there greeted me profusely. I think I must have been one of their first prospects. After I inquired about their services, the manager said that to come over and evaluate our needs would cost $90; if we decided to hire them, it would be something like $100 per day. I gulped, thanked them, and quickly left.

From then on, I simply relied on my earlier post-college library training, my instincts, and my knowledge of A.A. Several years later, in the middle seventies, I attended a course at the National Archives in Washington, D.C., and was pleased to find I had instinctively made most of the right moves in organizing the material. Long before we left 305 East Forty-fifth, I had collected much of the important categories, including the *Grapevines*, conference reports, newsletters, directories, correspondence (Bill's and Dr. Bob's and the groups'), G.S.O. records, A.A. World Service directors' meetings, trustees' meetings, conferences and conventions, financial records, and so forth. But it was only a beginning of the overall categories that needed to be collected, systematized, and preserved.

I continued this collecting and organizing for the next fifteen years, mostly on my own, but with Bill's constant encouragement, until his death. Keeping up with his and my other office duties in the sixties made it a busy era. Before I retired, I came across letters written around 1957 by Bill to early A.A. friends around the country, on which I had written notes like, "Save the history records in your area because we're going to put them together in an archive." Apparently I didn't create any stampede in that direction for a long time.

In fact, there wasn't a lot of enthusiasm for this effort from anyone. For example, I had collected and carefully stored all of Bill's dictation tapes, as I finished them, including long memos to trustees on important issues, correspondence with well-known friends, and the like. These were a priceless, irreplaceable record, because they preserved his voice, explaining his important ideas, plans, proposals, and decisions from the fifties on. When the office moved in 1970 from Forty-fifth Street to its present location at 468 Park Avenue South, all these tapes were apparently destroyed. I never found them after the cabinet and contents were moved from the old location. I was, and still am, angry about that.

The problem was to try to guide people as to what *should* be preserved for the future. I kept stressing the necessity for it. A former manager reminded me of an order given some years earlier authorizing all group correspondence older than two years to be discarded for a lack of storage space. In the nick of time, I fussed about it, rescued the old group folders, and had them sent upstairs to me so I could decide what needed to be kept.

One beloved and perceptive old-timer did indeed understand the necessity of preserving A.A.'s history: Tom S., one of the earliest members in Jacksonville, Florida, and a past trustee. On his visits to the office in the sixties, we would chat about the preservation job (especially concerning Florida history). On each visit he would ask me how I was coming along, and I would tell him that though I was making headway in a minimal way, I had many other duties around the office as well. I was literally working seven days a week.

One day in early 1972, after not seeing Tom for two or three years, I had another nice chat with him about our favorite subject, the preservation project. About fifteen minutes after he left, in dashed Bob H., the general manager. "Now, Nell," he said. "Drop everything else you are doing and get right on the archives." And that's the way I became official archivist.

I learned soon afterward that Tom had gone directly to Bob after leaving my office, saying emphatically, "While Nell is still with us, we'd better get her going on those archives." I could only think I must have aged considerably in those two or three years since last seeing Tom.

Not long afterward, partly because of Tom S.'s great interest and partly because we loved him and enjoyed being in touch, we asked him to chair a subcommittee of early members to obtain personal stories and memoirs from them. We also asked them for any other histories or stories they could recommend. Connecting with local members spurred the states and provinces to create their own local archives.

With the move to Park Avenue South in 1970, the history records, together with boxes of material not yet examined from our old "writing & research" days, were stored in the big room Bill and I shared as an office. After he died, the room was partitioned into two offices for other people to use. I was moved across the corridor to a tiny little cave of a room, with my files stacked so high around me visitors didn't realize there was a body sitting at a desk behind that tower of boxes.

But it didn't stay that way. I reported to Bob's administrative assistant, Midge M. With her valuable help, the following year the archives was given its own space on the newly-leased eighth floor. My desk was in a large, sunny corner room with pale blue walls and pumpkin-colored chairs. The floor was carpeted and we had attractive lamps. This office was flanked on one side by a small workroom and on the other by a sizable storage room. We finally had official recognition and status.

For a while, we engaged a professional librarian, Edith Klein, as a consultant to help me catalogue the material in a library format. However, I soon learned there was a vast difference between a library and an archival setup. Nevertheless, Edith's assistance was important and helpful to us.

I also acquired a much-needed secretary and general assistant—Harriet G. Her sponsor knew some of the staff at G.S.O. and Harriet was referred to our office for temporary work answering the sympathy letters and cards that arrived after Bill died. When this was finished, we engaged her for part-time work as my assistant. Harriet left because of illness in the late seventies, but we remained devoted friends and saw each other regularly until her death in May 1986.

Another assistant who is still a close friend is Sheila T. Sheila joined Harriet and me in the middle seventies. Though she didn't stay around as long as Harriet, I am still grateful for her time with the archives and for her contributions.

Harriet and Sheila were followed by a couple of other assistants and clerks over the years. Meanwhile, Frank M. had joined G.S.O. as administrative assistant to the general manager, Midge having retired. It turned out that among his many qualities, including a deep spirituality and a remarkable ability to share his A.A. experience passionately and articulately, was a great interest in A.A. history. On the organization chart, I reported to Frank, who also served (as Midge had) as secretary of our Trustees' Archives Committee. He took a closer and closer interest in the archives until the end of 1982, when he took over as archivist when I retired.

In 1973, the year following my appointment as archivist, the General Service Board of A.A. created the Trustees' Archives Committee as a standing committee of the board. The committee held its first meeting on October 24, 1973. There were three members: George G., chairman, professor of communications at Hofstra University; Rev. Lee Belford; and Dr. Milton Maxwell, the long-contributing nonalcoholic trustee who later became chairman of the board. He died in October 1988. Midge M., administrative assistant to the general manager, served as secretary of the committee, and I was also present. At that first meeting the purpose of the committee was clearly stated: "To keep the record straight so that myth does not predominate over fact as to historical accuracy."

We developed our own budget requirements for office furniture, card catalogue, framing of historic pictures and documents, display cases, visual equipment, and other necessities. The committee also considered questions of policy, including overall classifications of all material and who would have access to the different classifications. It encouraged and helped area archives to develop, and granted permission to reprint from uncopyrighted archival records. The Trustees' Archives Committee has continued to meet on at least a quarterly basis ever since. The size has increased from three members to six.

My first project as archivist, which occupied the entire summer of 1972, was to integrate Bill's correspondence files, which I had maintained at Stepping Stones over the years, with those I maintained at the G.S.O. Later, Lois contributed valuable items from her own files such as a duplicate of an early scrapbook, letters between her and Bill when he was in Akron in 1935, and her own diaries dating from 1937 through 1954. Bill and Dr. Bob's letters remain an important category of the archives.

A second category of archival material is the group history correspondence files started in the first twenty years. These tell how the groups got started and how they grew in different parts of the U.S. and Canada and overseas.

The third broad category is the General Service Office records, starting with the business records and history of the old Alcoholic Foundation, Works Publishing, Inc., and the Headquarters office, as we called it in the forties.

Still another category covers photographs, displays, maps, awards, scrapbooks, citations, art, tapes, cassettes, books, and other miscellaneous items.

Most of the important early material was microfilmed, beginning in the middle seventies and the microfilms were coded, labeled, and indexed for easy retrieval. At the same time, we undertook to record on cassette tapes the significant talks we had accumulated on wire recordings, phonograph records, and other obsolete recording formats. All microfilms and cassettes were done in duplicate, with the second copy stored in a storage vault in New Jersey.

The archives also has oral histories from long-time members as well as area and state histories on tape or in written form. Collecting these is an ongoing activity, but I am grateful that we have preserved the memories of many members who have passed on in recent years.

128

Again, the archives is not a library. While the visitor today will indeed see bookcases containing one copy of every printing of the Big Book and subsequent books, and a wall of bookshelves containing books on alcoholism and books either mentioning A.A. or written by A.A. members, he or she will also see an array of pictures on the wall and a variety of memorabilia and historical artifacts. One wall is covered with photos of Bill and Lois and early A.A. scenes in New York. Another has photos of Dr. Bob and Anne, Sister Ignatia, and A.A. locations in Akron. A third wall has crowd photos from all the international conventions since 1955. Visitors will also see the Lasker Award, Dr. Carl Jung's famous letter to Bill, and other museum objects.

Several attractions in the archives are all-time favorites with visitors. One is the carefully preserved first copy of the first printing of the first edition of the Big Book. A slightly oversize volume with a red-colored cloth binding, it is a gift from the widow of Jim B., one of the first ten members of A.A. in the eastern U.S., even before it was called A.A. The book bears a handwritten notation by Jim B. as to its authenticity, and the signatures of scores of early members.

Other prime attractions are the fifteen large scrapbooks of early newspaper clippings about A.A. Newsprint deteriorates and crumbles to pieces over the years, so the original scrapbooks from the early years were in dreadful condition. We sent them to a first-rate restoration firm in New York, which did a laborious but amazing job. It involved soaking the clippings to deacidify them, then carefully drying and remounting them on acid-free paper. Each page was then encapsulated in mylar before being rebound in durable covers, in chronological order.

It is a very expensive procedure, but well worth it

because the finished scrapbooks not only provide a unique picture of A.A.'s growth from 1939 on, but they also show how the public regarded alcoholism and how newspaper writers reported on the new Fellowship. The language they used is amusing today; for example, consider the headline, "A.A.s Battle Demon Rum."

Our 1939-42 scrapbook carries headlines like: "Rockefeller Dines Toss-Pots," or "Secretary Helps Chronic Drunks," or "Bared as Angel of Reform Project." Another: "Former Topers Plan to Aid New Crop." And later: "Try an Abstinence Cocktail with Alcoholics Anonymous." The editors loved the term "Water Wagon," as in "Life on the Water Wagon Extolled" or, referring to Bill, "Water Wagon Head Visits Here."

The devices used to protect anonymity at the media level in those days bring a laugh today. One full-page newspaper photo shows a man wearing a Halloween mask to protect his anonymity. Several other pictures show an audience holding handkerchiefs in front of their faces. Another shows two members wearing masks like Lone Rangers.

Soon after the archives was established in New York, local archives began to appear, which we encouraged as an important corollary to our own efforts at G.S.O. Some of the earlier ones in the U.S. were in southern California, Washington state, Utah, Florida, Chicago, Missouri, Arizona, and Washington, DC. Early ones in Canada were in Ontario, Quebec, and British Columbia. Today, there are 180 archival centers in the U.S. and Canada and in ten countries overseas. Periodically, our archives distributes a newsletter called *Markings* to share helpful information among other archive centers in the field.

We have also explored ways of sharing our materials with them and with the rest of the Fellowship as well.

Available, for example, is a copy of the original manuscript of the Big Book, sometimes called the "multilith" copy. A full-size copy of the earliest of the scrapbooks is available and more items are planned. Tapes of important talks by the cofounders can be purchased. Sets of prints of historic photos are also available for framing.

Probably the most effective tool we have for taking the archives to the Fellowship is the filmstrip *Markings on the Journey*, prepared at the initiative of Mike R. when he was chairman of the Trustees' Archives Committee around 1979 and unveiled at the New Orleans Convention in 1980. I wasn't completely in favor of this idea originally, but I quickly changed my mind as the project began. We owe a debt of gratitude to a number of people, especially Mike R. The filmstrip isn't just about the archives; it tells the story of the first fifteen years of A.A. plus highlights of later history. You hear Bill and Dr. Bob's voices, and see such early nonalcoholic friends as Sister Ignatia, Fr. Dowling, Harry Tiebout, Bernard Smith, and Sam Shoemaker.

The biographies of the two cofounders published by A.A.—*Dr. Bob and the Good Oldtimers* and *Pass It On*— owe much to the archival material as well.

But there was at least one embarrassing moment. The official ribbon-cutting ceremonies to open the archives were held on November 3, 1975, immediately following the meeting of the General Service Board so that most of the trustees could be there, as well as a sizable crowd of other interested guests. Chairman George G. presided, and Lois, Dr. Jack Norris, and Tom S. all made brief remarks. George, during his opening remarks, was kind enough to say, "I'll never again hear the words 'labor of love' without thinking of Nell." That moved me very much, and still does. Lois and Tom S. cut a blue ribbon to symbolize the availability of the archives. The ceremony was photographed, but after the food and coffee were served, the assembled group had their laugh of the day: we suddenly realized that we had totally forgotten to tape the historic ceremony for posterity.

In 1981 the archives department was again moved as part of a major refurbishing and expansion of G.S.O. The present site is on the fifth floor of 468 Park Avenue South. There is a large central room devoted entirely to exhibits and memorabilia except for a receptionist/clerk's desk. A research room contains a conference table along with a large library of books, bound scrapbooks, and other material. Frank M., our present archivist, and his assistant share another room, where the area histories are filed, and off this space is a good-sized storeroom where the confidential material is housed. A receptionist/ secretary sits in the main reception room.

Soon after I became archivist in the early seventies, I began receiving invitations to share some A.A. history at A.A. conferences, conventions, and other get-togethers in the U.S. and Canada—even in Bristol, England, thanks to good friend Travers C., himself concerned with preparing the record of his country. Travers died in October 1990 after many years spent carrying the A.A. message at home and abroad.

Sometimes groups wanted to hear memories of Bill and Lois and stories about the early days. Sometimes they wanted more information about the archives. Other times, the subjects were anonymity or humor in A.A.

After turning over the reins of the archives to Frank M., I retired from Alcoholics Anonymous at the end of 1982, at the age of 65, but have kept in close touch ever since.

13

LOIS W.: GREAT LADY, DEAR FRIEND

So be my passing!
My task accomplished and the long day done
My wages taken, and in my heart some late
lark singing
Let me be gathered to the quiet West
The sundown splendid and serene, Death

These words from the poem "Margaritoe Sorori" by
W. E. Henley have come to me often during the sad months
that have passed since Lois' death on October 5, 1988, at the
age of 97½. They remind me poignantly of her—of her
inner strength, energy, and courage in confronting and deal-
ing with many of life's problems right up to the end.

If you were to ask me Lois' most characteristic trait, I
would say it was her love of home. She always remained
home-oriented, and after the spring of 1941, home was Stepping Stones in Bedford Hills, New York. Being creative, she
took great satisfaction in decorating and painting the rooms,
cutting and sewing all the draperies and chair covers, and
making many of her own clothes on the same machine.

We enjoyed our Scrabble™ games, which went back many years. We made up our own rules, and created our own dictionary, which we were constantly adding to. Crossword puzzles were also a favorite.

Lois was an artist and had studied at the New York School of Fine and Applied Art. She drew all her own illustrations for her book, *Lois Remembers*. And she loved to design her own Christmas cards, with variations from year to year. For many years I would help her prepare for the mailing, starting on weekends in November. We usually sent 300 cards and more in later years.

Perhaps her talent for drawing related to her ability, as she described many times, to *observe*. She often said that she just didn't *see* or *look* at things, she observed them, a trait I admired very much, and which I've tried to develop myself. A day doesn't pass that I don't observe patterns or objects as I walk around our beautiful garden-like housing project here in the middle of New York City.

Lois was musical. She liked to listen to classical music and played the piano very well herself.

Lois loved children. Years ago, several small youngsters in the neighborhood visited her regularly. At Halloween, Lois set the table with lots of candy and trinkets. At Thanksgiving, she gave away pumpkins from the garden to the children, who drew straws to see who would get the largest one.

Later on, as the youngsters grew into their teens, a couple of the boys in the neighborhood asked for permission to create a motorcycle path around the property. Lois had a long-standing affinity for motorcycles, so she gave her permission gladly. Over the next two or three years, we all had to get used to the roar of machines circling the grounds once or twice a day.

When she was in her nineties, Lois was a speaker at the Desert Roundup, an A.A. convention in California. As she was being pushed across the parking lot in her wheel-chair, she spied a huge, gleaming Harley Davidson motor-cycle and asked to be wheeled over to admire it. Once there, she asked to be photographed alongside it. (The photo is located upstairs at Stepping Stones.) When she was introduced for her talk the following day, the Motor-cycle Group of A.A. made her an honorary member. She loved it.

Like Bill, Lois was pragmatic as well as spiritual. She valued her privacy, but looked forward to and enjoyed visits from friends. She liked to entertain A.A., Al-Anon, and other friends at such annual events as her New Year's open house, the Al-Anon picnic, the tours of Stepping Stones by A.A. and Al-Anon delegates at their conference times, and holiday parties.

She was quick to share her "experience, strength, and hope" and her understanding of emotional problems. But on another level, she was a bit of a stoic, a noncomplainer, avoiding mentioning her own aches and pains. Much as she valued her privacy, she was also willing to travel among the A.A. groups around the country with Bill, talking to the spouses and family members. Then, in 1951, she took on a leadership role, along with Anne B., in structuring the Al-Anon Fellowship.

Back in the forties, at the A.A. General Service Office, we maintained a list of family members or groups who had written to us requesting help. From our files, we would provide them with names of similar groups, send them the pamphlet, *To Wives*—a reprint from the Big Book—and put them in touch with one another. By 1950, about the time Bill had persuaded Lois to organize the family side of the problem, we were listing some 85 to 90 groups. We turned these names over to Lois and Anne B., who contacted them and soon they had more work than they could handle.

In early 1952, they moved their activities away from Stepping Stones, first into the upstairs level of the Twenty-fourth Street Clubhouse in Manhattan, where they were better able to enlist volunteers, and then to an office on Twenty-third Street. Today, including Alateen, more than 30,000 groups exist worldwide.

In January 1954, Lois had a heart attack that alarmed all of us greatly. However, after a year of rest and recuperation—which she said she thoroughly enjoyed—she recovered completely. She never had a recurrence. Her first big outing was to attend the A.A. Convention in St. Louis, where she made a major address immediately following the famous "Coming of Age" ceremony. In fact, Lois attended and participated in every international convention from 1950 until her death in 1988.

In the late seventies, Lois bowed to pressure from many of her friends and wrote her autobiography, *Lois Remembers*. An A.A. friend and professional writer, Barry L., helped her organize the material and put it into publishable form, but the content, the writing, and even the illustrations are entirely and unmistakably Lois.

In her grief over the loss of Bill in 1971, Lois was supported by A.A. and Al-Anon members throughout the world. So she began thinking of taking a trip around the world to see them firsthand—something she and Bill had promised themselves that they would do "someday soon." The service offices of A.A. and Al-Anon in New York contacted various groups around the globe who in turn arranged meetings and offered hospitality.

In January 1972, accompanied by Evelyn C. from the Al-Anon office, Lois set out. Africa was their first stop where they visited Kenya and then Victoria Falls. They had a strenuous schedule of A.A. and Al-Anon meetings in Johannesburg, Durban, Port Elizabeth, and Capetown. Lois was pleased to see that these meetings were among the few occasions in South Africa where there was no separation of races.

She and Evelyn then visited the Fellowships in Australia and New Zealand and made contacts in Hong Kong and Japan. Their last stop was Honolulu.

Lois so enjoyed this experience that she continued to take many more trips, often inviting me to go along as her companion. In July 1972, we went on a cruise to see the solar eclipse off the coast of Nova Scotia. In March 1973, we went to London. In April 1974, we enjoyed the seventeenth all-Irish convention in Cork, Ireland, with Jack M., editor of the *Grapevine*. A dramatic moment was when our car was stopped at the border to Northern Ireland and guns were poked into the windows as our driver explained why we were there and where we were going.

We participated in the second Ocean Roundup (or "Cruise Without Booze," as it was more often called), a lovely weekend cruise—complete with meetings— from Miami to the Bahamas and back, planned and executed by Al S. in 1977.

Lois took two memorable trips to Washington, D.C. The first was when she was invited by Joe Hirshhorn, Bill's old business friend from his Wall Street days, to the opening of the Hirshhorn Museum of Art. Then in April 1985, Lois, her secretary, Fran, her close friend Doris McCormick and I traveled to Washington where we attended the National Council on Alcoholism Forum Luncheon and Lois was presented with their President's Award.

In February 1980, we went to Bermuda for a week at the invitation of Irving and Julie Harris for a nostalgic

137

visit with them and to stay in an old Oxford Group community in Somerset. I remember one quite unexpected afternoon event. Lois and I had just returned around four o'clock to the rooming house lobby and saw a small crowd gathered in the sitting room. Thinking we were just in time for tea we hastened to join the people seated around a large table but quickly realized it wasn't a tea party going on, but an Oxford Group-type meeting. We were greeted warmly and it was a memorable experience.

In June 1981 we attended the 25th Anniversary A.A. Convention in Switzerland. While there, we made a side visit to the Jung Institute in Zurich.

Lois began to fail physically in late 1985, forcing cancellation of our reservations for a special trip up the Amazon River, the climax of which was to see Halley's Comet make its spectacular dash across the heavens. Lois had seen this same event happen 76 years earlier, and relished the thought of seeing it twice in a lifetime, something the local newspapers picked up on. She mentioned her plan to almost every visitor at Stepping Stones, her eyes twinkling with merriment when their faces betrayed the predictable shock. But by autumn, it became apparent that she could not endure the trip. Her travel adventures were over. She wanted me to make the trip anyway, but I didn't want to go without her.

Although Lois turned 80 the year Bill died, she insisted on living on at Stepping Stones alone. Her daytime cook / housekeeper, Harriet, worked part-time days and the same on Saturday until her termination, so Lois wasn't totally by herself. I continued my regular schedule of visits and we kept up our walks when the weather was good. In addition to Lois' active involvement in Al-Anon, her many speaking engagements all over the country, her travels, and her various activities and interests, she had many visitors from all parts of the world.

The thing we most feared about Lois' living independently was that she would fall and injure herself with no one to help her. And, indeed, as she became more frail, she did have several falls, incurring fractures. One time, all alone, she fell from the second-floor stairway all the way down the winding staircase to the ground floor, landing right beside the telephone. The same thing happened another time when she fell in the downstairs bedroom, again within reach of the phone.

Lois was pragmatic, so she faced the necessity of structuring the remainder of her days so that she might live comfortably, graciously, and with dignity in her own home. She was helped immeasurably in late 1982 when she received a letter from a young man in Boston, an A.A. member named Francis H. He wrote that he had read her book and was concerned for her welfare. "You need help, and I can give you afternoons," he said.

Lois interviewed him and he came to work at Stepping Stones in January 1983, first as a caretaker and then as her secretary. He remained devoted to her until the end of her life.

After a couple of years of trial and error, she assembled a household staff of wonderful, devoted people. Besides Fran, there was Doris, who, with her husband, lived for a short time in the "new house" on the property, built for an anticipated caretaker. And there was Lois' daytime aide, Ethel Dumas, who Lois dubbed "Eternal Ethel." There was an afternoon aide, Carrie, as well as an all-night aide, Marge. She also relied on weekend relief aides, a cook, a caretaker-gardener, and, when needed, a driver. Fran H. took on the responsibility of being the archivist for Lois and Stepping Stones, employing an assistant to catalogue

139

the letters, manuscripts, and memorabilia that abound there. Ann Burnham Smith, Lois' second cousin, also visited on weekends. She was a great friend and a comfort to Lois.

There were two other outside people who were enormously helpful to Lois. The first was her dedicated friend and attorney Michael Alexander. Michael's association with Bill and Lois went all the way back to his early days as a junior member of Bernard Smith's law firm when Bern and Bill were designing A.A.'s General Service Conference. Upon Bern's death, Michael became general counsel for both Alcoholics Anonymous and Al-Anon and was, from 1976 to 1985, a Trustee of A.A. He was called back in 1988 to become Chairman of the Board.

Equally dedicated was Owen J. "Bud" Flanagan, Lois' accountant and financial advisor. Like Michael, Bud's association with A.A. went back to his youth when his boss, Wilbur "Bur" S., was the outside accountant for the headquarters office. Bud continues that relationship today. Both Michael and Bud helped Lois find a way to preserve Stepping Stones for the benefit of A.A. and Al-Anon visitations and activities after her death. From the time of Bill's death, this was one of Lois' prime concerns. After the two Fellowships had to decline acceptance of the property as a gift, because of A.A.'s Sixth Tradition, Lois decided to establish a foundation to be administered by an outside board of trustees. She shared with Michael and Bud her ideas for maintaining the grounds, property, and buildings after her death and also thoughts we often spoke about, such as making meaningful contributions to alcoholism treatment with better-trained nurses, doctors, and others.

I'd like to let Mike explain the early Foundation activity in his own words:

> Those discussions led to the incorporation of the Stepping Stones Foundation in 1979 as a nonprofit corporation under the laws of the State of New York. From its inception, the Foundation was positioned to receive the Stepping Stones property as a gift from Lois, the principal purpose for which it was formed. Meanwhile, the foundation became "active" in order to obtain and maintain a tax-exempt status that was important to its funding needs.
>
> The interim activities of the Foundation, those between its incorporation and the death of Lois, were funded by annual gifts from Lois. It was understood that the main funding of the Foundation would come from Lois in the form of a bequest of royalties derived from the sale of A.A. books authored by Bill. Lois did indeed bequeath a major part of those royalties to the foundation to provide for the essential needs of Stepping Stones.

The original directors of the Foundation were Lois, Dr. Lyman Burnham (Lois' brother), Henrietta S. (retired from Al-Anon), and myself. The number of directors increased over the years but Lois remained active as its President and Chairman of the Board until her death.

With the Foundation established, Lois sailed into her nineties with zest and good humor. She continued to attend—and to speak at—every opening dinner of the A.A. and Al-Anon annual general service conferences, every annual "Bill's Birthday Dinner" in New York, and every international convention. And she continued to accept invitations to speak at other conventions and

141

conferences of the Fellowships such as the annual Founders' Day in Akron, which she especially enjoyed.

In October 1982, at age 91, she invited as many A.A. members as we could contact who had sobered up prior to 1950 to an Old-Timers' Day at Stepping Stones. It was a good-sized, exciting affair, with a large yellow-and-white striped tent set up outside, a catered meal, and perhaps 100 to 150 guests. Among them were Doctor Bob's son and daughter—Bob S. and Sue Windows—and their spouses, perhaps the only two people alive today who were there when Bill and Bob began the A.A. program.

Lois personally handled everything from the invitations to chairing a kind of group meeting that was held in the large living room. Everyone shared something of his or her early experience, and Barry L. presented Lois, on behalf of the group, a lovely amethyst and gold ring to replace at long last the engagement ring from Bill lost early in their marriage. Lois enjoyed the whole event tremendously.

Even as she became weaker, more feeble, and physically smaller, Lois' mind remained amazingly sharp. At her open house and other parties at Stepping Stones, she made a point of greeting every guest, inquiring about their families, and often carrying on long conversations with old friends among them. She continued to be interviewed occasionally by the press and to receive visitors frequently. She enjoyed afternoon drives around the countryside with Fran or Ron (the caretaker) at the wheel. Right up to the end, she liked to go out for lunch on her birthday and other special occasions—and sometimes for no occasion at all.

Lois was present as usual—with Fran H. and myself— as guests of A.A. at a dinner in the grand ballroom of the Hotel Roosevelt at the opening of the General Service

Conference in April 1988. As she was being introduced, she was wheeled to the stage and helped to the microphone, a tiny, frail figure, her gray head barely visible above the lectern. But she delivered her greeting in a remarkably strong voice and ended with, "I'll see you next year." The audience cheered as they rose. In September, she twinkled her weak eyes at a visitor and told him, "I'm going to make 100, you know."

But she didn't, quite. When I was at Stepping Stones the weekend of September 16 to 18, 1988, she was breathing with difficulty. Both Claudette, her weekend aide at that time, and I thought she should be in the hospital. When we called her doctor, he was unable to see her at that time, but after listening to Claudette describe Lois' condition over the phone, he directed her to increase her medication and promised to check her on Monday. Calmed down by the doctor's advice, I returned to New York on my usual train Sunday evening.

The next day I learned early that she had been taken to Northern Westchester Hospital, where she was in intensive care. During that week, she had to be connected by nose tube to a breathing apparatus. However, when we visited her, she was in good spirits, able to talk, with her sharp good humor not a bit diminished. She was even taken back home on Saturday, at the end of that first week, but was rushed back to the hospital later that same day and endured the presence of a throat tube connected to a respirator by her bedside and other life-support equipment. For the next week and a half she was again in intensive care.

This was a more difficult time for Lois. It was harder for her to sit up, she couldn't speak, of course, and we were aware of a further physical decline. She communicated by writing on a pad as best she could. She recognized visitors, and her mind and her sense of humor were still sharp.

It was during these last days that John B., then general manager of the G.S.O., called on her in the hospital. He expressed his personal gratitude and that of the Fellowship because, he told her, "A.A.s owe their lives to you." A ghost of a smile crossed Lois' features and she wrote on her pad, "Not to me, to God." John replied, "But you are His servant." And Lois wrote, "So are you."

By the beginning of the third week, Lois had contracted pneumonia, and on Wednesday, October 5, the doctor replaced the throat tube with a transparent face mask. An hour later, Ethel, Ann, and myself, standing at her bedside, remarked on how peaceful she looked, eyes open, her hands soft and warm. Since all seemed well for a while, and Ethel and Ann Smith were also with Lois, I went to get a quick sandwich. Although I was gone only two or three minutes, Lois left us in that brief interval or perhaps already had. She died about 3:15 p.m., Wednesday, October 5, 1988.

Ethel said afterward, "This lady always knew what she wanted." Earlier that afternoon, Lois wrote on her pad, "want to sleep." "And," said Ethel, "that's just what she did."

The next day, Fran, Ann, and I met with the funeral director. We set the date for the graveside burial service in East Dorset, Vermont, on October 10, with a memorial service in New York City on October 20.

Obituaries appeared in the New York Times and other newspapers throughout the country, and, of course, lengthy obituaries appeared in A.A. and Al-Anon publications. Michael Alexander announced her death in a letter to the A.A. Fellowship. It said in part:

In the early days the entire future of our Fellowship and of countless alcoholics hung on the
thread of the determination of Bill W. and Dr.
Bob to put Alcoholics Anonymous on firm
ground. Lois Wilson is regarded by many as
someone without whom her husband could not
have persisted in that crucial work. Bill referred
to her as a "full partner" in the struggles and
joys of those early days.

On October 8, the Saturday afternoon after Lois' death,
about 50 family and friends gathered for an informal,
Quaker-style service in the living room at Stepping Stones.
At Fran's request, I presided, standing before a roaring fire
in the stone fireplace. After I had shared briefly some of
my own memories of her, others rose and spoke as the
spirit moved them. Michael Alexander sounded a note
that I have tried to express here; namely, Lois' many
talents and many sides. She was not only the cofounder
and guiding force of Al-Anon, but a writer, photographer,
artist, poet, musician, and, in her later years, an effective
speaker, and a lover of nature.

Others shared poignant, bittersweet, even funny memories of her indomitable spirit, her sharp mind, her sense of
humor, and her feistiness. Ralph B., a writer for the old
Alcoholic Foundation and a frequent visitor to Stepping
Stones from the earliest days, said she was "a force that
kept everything going while Bill was thinking or writing or
visualizing." He continued, "I would sometimes stand up
to Bill, but I wouldn't think of arguing with Lois."

On October 20, 1988, a memorial service, arranged by
the Al-Anon Family Group Headquarters, was held at the
Marble Collegiate Church in New York made famous by
the ministry of Norman Vincent Peale, who knew and
admired both Bill and Lois and Alcoholics Anonymous.

Among those who participated were Robert D., chairman, Al-Anon's Board of Trustees and Myrna H., executive director of Al-Anon, John B. from A.A., Fran H., and myself. Judy C. sang the beautiful and moving "Amazing Grace" and James G. contributed "The Lord's Prayer" set to music. The large church was filled for the service. In his eulogy, the minister, Dr. Arthur Caliandro, remarked on how unusual it was for such a huge crowd to turn out for the funeral of a 97-year-old person, and how it symbolized her larger family, the family of many millions who had lived new lives because of her work. I count myself one of them.

14

WHAT A.A. MEANS TO ME

Some years back, I was worried about a heart murmur, which turned out to be nothing serious. I was being examined by a young female physician. She asked me what I did, and I told her that, though a nonalcoholic, I had worked for A.A. for many years. Her face brightened up and she declared, "Oh, I know all about the Twelve Steps. I'm not an alcoholic either, but the Steps are important in my life."

I knew exactly what she meant, because I've tried to do the same thing; that is, try to face reality squarely and honestly—at least most of the time. I continually apply A.A. principles to the moral and ethical decisions I have to make. As Bill would say, "Thus we grow."

For example, during postoperative recovery in the hospital a few years ago, I was able to pass on this way of life to others. And that brings an added dimension of joy and gratitude to my life.

Today there are so many members of Alcoholics Anonymous and Al-Anon, not to mention the other Twelve Step programs, plus relatives and friends whose lives have been touched and changed dramatically, that I feel A.A. is changing the world. When I said that to Bill years ago, he laughed and said, "You can say that," meaning that he could not, and he repeatedly cautioned the Fellowship about such grandiose thinking.

Nevertheless, I am not alone among nonalcoholics who feel this way about the A.A. way of life. I've heard Michael Alexander say that just by being associated with the Fellowship "you grow and mature." And Dr. Jack Norris said, "We are all selfish and irritable and resentful at times. But A.A. shows us how to get rid of these defects of character that ruin our relationships."

From the beginning, I was caught by the A.A. Fellowship, specifically by the caring. It was not so much a general "caring for our fellowman," but a one-on-one caring, a love for one another without thought of any reward. An acceptance. The instant, unspoken communication is unique. That's one reason people are drawn to A.A., knowing instinctively, I'm sure, that this reaching out, this loving recognition, is the essence of spirituality, the root of the Being in all of us. That's how I interpret A.A.

And, of course, a practical reason for A.A.'s success is that the Fellowship implements and promotes further growth and maturity after the alcoholic has quit drinking.

The principles of A.A. helped me when I realized I had to stop smoking. I had tried to stop many times since 1966, and it was at this time that Bill started using a hand inhalator for his breathing difficulty. But over the next three years, watching Bill continue to smoke and becoming steadily more frail with emphysema, I made my decision finally, on January 1, 1969, and haven't smoked since. One day at a time did it for me even though it wasn't easy.

As I have moved into my seventies, my life is rich and full, thanks to A.A. I have countless friends throughout the world with whom I am in touch regularly and who express their love and support for me, which I return full measure. I have been invited to share at meetings where I'm given much more credit than I deserve. Because I, too, try to practice the Steps, I have been and am able to cope with unforeseen realities such as cancer, or the death of dear friends, as well as occasional personal conflicts, with some degree of courage, forthrightness, and honesty— instead of running away or avoiding them as I used to.

I am especially grateful for the precious friendship of Bill and Lois, as well as the many other A.A. friends, present and departed, who have brought such meaning to my life. I realize, however, that I am only one small example of what is happening on a tremendous scale every day; namely, the Fellowships of Alcoholics Anonymous and Al-Anon continuing to bestow upon alcoholics, their families and friends, and other troubled people, or those in need of spiritual guidance, their healing and ever-renewing benefactions.

NOTES

1. *Alcoholics Anonymous Comes of Age* (New York: Alcoholics Anonymous Publishing Inc., 1957), p. 181.

2. Ibid.

3. Ibid.

4. *Dr. Bob and the Good Oldtimers* (New York: Alcoholics Anonymous World Services, Inc., 1980), p. 202.

5. Bill Wilson, *Twelve Concepts for World Service by Bill W.* (New York: Alcoholics Anonymous World Services, Inc., 1962), p. 6.

6. Jessica Bové, "From the Outside Looking In," *The A.A. Grapevine* (New York: The A.A. Grapevine, Inc.) 2, no. 9 (February 1946): p. 8.

7. Ibid.

8. Ibid.

9. *The Language of the Heart: Bill W.'s Grapevine Writings* (New York: Alcoholics Anonymous World Services, Inc./A.A. Grapevine, Inc., 1988), p. 13.

10. Ibid., p. 18.

11. *Alcoholics Anonymous Comes of Age*, p. 232.

12. *Pass It On: The Story of Bill Wilson and How the A.A. Message Reached the World* (New York: Alcoholics Anonymous World Services, Inc., 1984), p. 278.

13. Ibid., p. 84.

14. *Alcoholics Anonymous Comes of Age*, p. 5.

15. *The Co-Founders of Alcoholics Anonymous: Brief Biographies of A.A.'s First Two Members* (New York: Alcoholics Anonymous World Services, Inc., 1972).

16. Ibid.

17. "The Anecdote Bin," *The A.A. Grapevine*, 21, no. 1 (June 1964): p. 33.

18. "Once Over Lightly," *The A.A. Grapevine*, 27, no. 9 (February 1971): p. 33.

19. *The A.A. Grapevine*, 24, no. 1 (June 1967): p. 19.